DISCOVER QGIS

THE WORKBOOK FOR THE AWARD WINNING GEOACADEMY CURRICULUM

PART 1 – INTRODUCTION TO GEOSPATIAL TECHNOLOGY

KURT MENKE, GISP

Credits & Copyright

Discover QGIS

PART 1 – INTRODUCTION TO GEOSPATIAL TECHNOLOGY

by Kurt Menke, GISP

Published by Locate Press LLC

COPYRIGHT © 2016 LOCATE PRESS LLC
ISBN: 978-0989421775
ALL RIGHTS RESERVED.

Direct permission requests to info@locatepress.com or mail:
Locate Press LLC, PO Box 671897, Chugiak, AK, USA, 99567-1897

Editor   Gary Sherman
Cover Design   Julie Springer
Interior Design   Based on Memoir-LaTeXdocument class
Publisher Website   http://locatepress.com
Book Website   http://locatepress.com/dqw

Contents

Editor's Note

This book contains content covering the first topic of the full *Discover QGIS* book.

Discover QGIS has 472 pages, covering five topics:

1. Introduction to Geospatial Technology (this book)
2. Spatial Analysis
3. Data Acquisition and Management
4. Cartographic Design
5. Remote Sensing

You can learn more about *Discover QGIS* and other titles at `http://locate.press`.

Foreword

It is with great pleasure I introduce you to Discover QGIS by Kurt Menke. This volume is the result of our collaboration for a decade to promote the adoption of open source software by geospatial educators and industry professionals. It reflects Kurt's deep technical knowledge and his extensive teaching experience. Kurt has long been a beacon of hope for open source advocates who share in the community of practice of QGIS and open source software. His extensive GIS consulting experience around his home base of Albuquerque, New Mexico and involvement in national healthcare and conservation societies, is reflected in Discover QGIS. He applies the geospatial technology skills defined in the US Department of Labor's Geospatial Technology Model (GTCM) to practical exercises in each of the chapters.

Kurt's decades of university, college and private teaching experience, only reinforce the quality of his pedagogical approach to the volume. In the field of geospatial technology education, his book adds greatly to the sparsely available collection of print volumes, and we will all benefit greatly from Discover QGIS for years to come. I look forward to its adoption by our GeoAcademy learners in 2016.

Phillip Davis, Ed.D
Director, GeoAcademy
Professor of Computer Science
Computer Science, Engineering and Advanced Technology Department
Del Mar College, Corpus Christi Texas, USA

About this Book

The GeoAcademy was founded in 2013, when Dr. Phil Davis brought together subject matter experts to author the first ever GIS curriculum based on a national standard—the U.S. Department of Labor's Geospatial Competency Model (GTCM). The GTCM is a hierarchical model of the knowledge, skills, and abilities (KSA's) needed to be a working GIS professional in today's marketplace. These KSA's were vetted by forty U.S. college GIS educators. Since 95% of U.S based colleges and universities use a single vendor's GIS software, it was decided the GeoAcademy should be built using free and open source software (FOSS4G). Over the summer of 2014 the exercises were beta tested on Canvas by over 3,000 students. The first edition of the GeoAcademy was released in September 2014. The GeoAcademy is therefore more of an attempt to teach GIS using QGIS, versus being a QGIS manual. (The GeoAcademy labs are licensed under the Creative Commons Attribution 3.0 Unported License. To view a copy of this license, visit http://creativecommons.org/licenses/by/3.0/)

Since its development, the GeoAcademy curriculum has been presented at several FOSS4G conferences and is being used by many professors in their GIS programs. An online GeoAcademy MOOC has over 5,000 enrollees. In 2015 the GeoAcademy team was honored to win the Global Educator of the Year Team Award by GeoForAll (http://www.geoforall.org/).

Now for the first time, this curriculum has been converted to fit into a convenient workbook format. Originally written for QGIS 2.4, the GeoAcademy material in this workbook has been updated for use with QGIS 2.14, Inkscape 0.91, and GRASS GIS 7.0.3. The material is also backwards compatible to QGIS v2.8 despite minor GUI changes. It therefore represents the most up-to-date version of the GeoAcademy curriculum.

This workbook covers GIS fundamentals, spatial analysis, data management, cartography and remote sensing. There are solution files for each exercise and most exercises have a challenge exercise. Discussion questions are also included at the end of each exercise. Some of the many highlights include learning how to: work with coordinate reference systems, create data via georeferencing and geocoding, using GRASS to conduct a supervised classification of satellite imagery, and how to work with both QGIS and Inkscape to create a publication quality map.

Thought was given to improving the content and organization for both hardcopy and electronic readers. The GeoAcademy data was reorganized to match the chapter structure of this book. Changes were made to several exercises, reflecting the newly updated integration of GRASS GIS with QGIS that came with QGIS v2.10. Portions that include working with GRASS vector maps include both GRASS 6 and GRASS 7 versions of the exercise databases. The portions using the free software Multi-Spec were rewritten using QGIS. Efforts were also made to incorporate some of the exciting new QGIS features such as Live Layer Effects into the Challenge Assignments.

It is my pleasure to work with Locate Press to bring this workbook into print and e-book formats so that more people can learn GIS with FOSS4G tools. I hope you enjoy the book!

The Data

The data for this book are available for download at http://locatepress.com/workbook/. They are organized by part and exercise. Each exercise includes solution files and answers to exercise questions.

About the Author

A former archaeologist, Kurt Menke is a Certified GIS Professional (GISP) based out of Albuquerque, New Mexico. He received a Master's degree in Geography from the University of New Mexico in 2000. That same year he founded Bird's Eye View (http://www.BirdsEyeViewGIS.com) to apply his expertise with GIS technology towards ecological conservation. Along with conservation, his other focus areas are public health and education. He is an avid open source GIS proponent, recently authoring Mastering QGIS for Packt Publishing. In 2015 he became an OsGeo Charter Member. He is an experienced FOSS4G educator and is a co-author of the GeoAcademy. In 2015 he was awarded the Global Educator of the Year Team Award by GeoForAll as part of the GeoAcademy team.

Acknowledgments

Each of the authors who contributed to these exercises is a very experienced GIS professional and I am grateful for all of their contributions. Dr. Richard (Rick) Smith (Texas A & M University – Corpus Christi) has been part of the GeoAcademy since day one, and is the original author for many of these exercises. Nate Jennings (City of Sacramento, UC Davis, Del Mar College and Sacramento City College) was the original author for the remote sensing labs. Dr. John van Hoesen performed quality checking on the GeoAcademy labs. Finally, none of this material would have been developed if it had not been for the leadership of Dr. Phil Davis (Del Mar College) who was the principal investigator for the GeoAcademy.

Part I

Introduction to Geospatial Technology

Exercise 1

Spatial Data Models

Objective – Explore and Understand Spatial Data Models

1.1 Introduction

In this exercise, you'll explore and manage geospatial data using two modules of the FOSS4G software QGIS: QGIS Browser and QGIS Desktop. QGIS Browser is an application designed to preview and manage geospatial data. It is analogous to Windows Explorer, but works specifically with geospatial datasets. QGIS Desktop is the companion application used to perform spatial analysis and make maps.

This exercise will also introduce you to the QGIS interface, which is used throughout the workbook. It is important to learn the concepts in this exercise as future exercises will require the skills covered in this exercise.

This exercise includes the following tasks:

- Task 1 – Learn to work with QGIS Browser.

- Task 2 – Become familiar with geospatial data models.

- Task 3 – Viewing geospatial data in QGIS Desktop.

1.2 Objective: Explore and Understand Geospatial Data Models

Geographic Information Systems model the real world with representations of objects such as lakes, roads and towns. Geospatial data models are the means used to represent these features. They are composed of two parts: spatial features and attributes that when combined, create a model of reality.

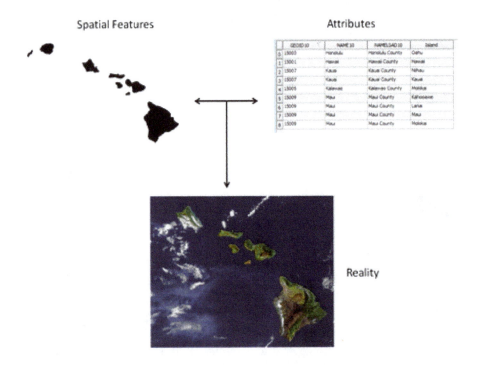

There are two main geospatial data models: vector and raster.

Vector Data Model – Best for modeling discrete objects. Vector data comes in three forms: point, line, and polygon.

Raster Data Model – This model is best for modeling continuous objects. A raster is composed of a matrix of contiguous cells, with each cell (pixel) holding a single numeric value.

1.3   Task 1 - Learn to Work with QGIS Browser

In this task, you will become familiar with QGIS Browser. The first step in working on a project with geospatial datasets is to organize your workspace. It is important that we organize datasets logically on the computer and make them easy to find. In this task, you will obtain a copy of the exercise data and explore how the data is organized using QGIS Browser.

Open QGIS Browser. The way you open QGIS Browser and QGIS Desktop will vary depending on your operating system. For this series of exercises, we will explain how to open and use QGIS using the Microsoft Windows 7 operating system.

1. Click Start | All Programs | QGIS | QGIS Browser.

The interface to QGIS Browser is simple and clean (shown in the figure below). The File Tree is displayed on the left, which shows your computer's files and folders. (NOTE: your machine may have a different set and number of drives listed here—this is fine.) Below the drives are Database Connections. There are no connections to any databases at this point. The Display Window takes up the remainder of the window. There are Display Tabs above the Display Window that allow you to control the information you see.

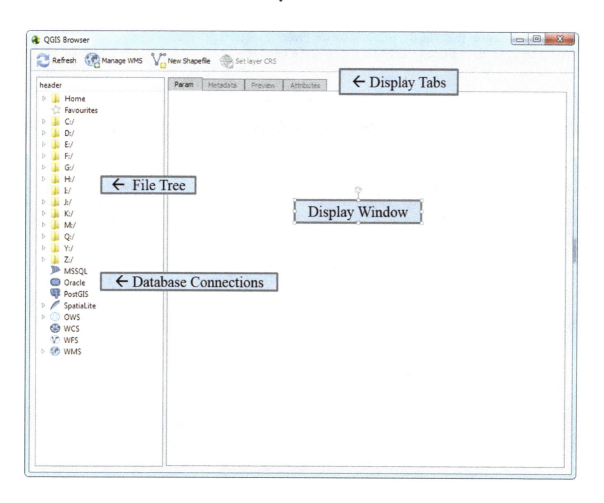

2. Look at the File Tree. Click the arrow to the left of the C: drive. You will now see all of the subfolders directly under the C:/ folder.

3. Expand the `Exercise 1 Data` folder where you stored your data in the File Tree by clicking the arrows to the left of each folder. You will now see the contents of the Data folder for the exercise (shown in figure below).

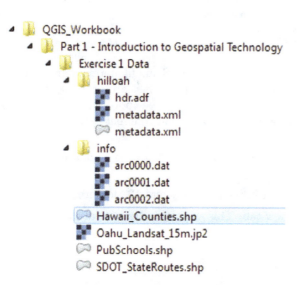

4. Take a moment to read the names of the files. There are two folders and several files listed with different

icons. The 🖾 icon indicates that the dataset is a vector layer. This icon ▓ is used to represent raster data but is also used for other files such as the XML files you see here.

1.4   Task 2 - Become Familiar with Geospatial Data Models

Now that you are familiar with the basic layout of QGIS Browser, we will explore some geospatial data.

1. Let's take a closer look at these data currently listed in QGIS Browser.

2. Select the `Hawaii_Counties.shp` layer in the File Tree. The Display Window automatically switches to the Metadata tab. This gives you some basic information about the dataset. You'll notice that the Storage type is ESRI shapefile. The Display Window also tells you that it has a Geometry type of polygon and it has 9 features (shown in figure below).

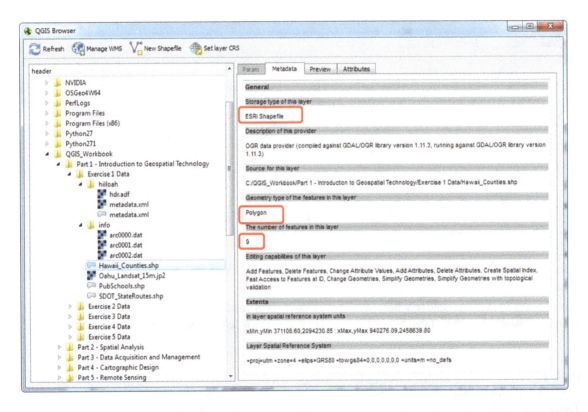

In addition to data models (vector and raster) we have to understand file formats. Some file formats are designed to store vector, and others raster data. Shapefiles are vector file format. In fact, they are probably the most common vector file format. An individual shapefile can only contain one geometry type (polygon, line, or point). A shapefile is actually a collection of files on the computer with a common name, but different extensions.

3. Now select `PubSchools.shp`. You'll see that this is also an ESRI Shapefile but that it is a point dataset with 287 features.

4. Select `SDOT_StateRoutes.shp`. This is an ESRI Shapefile with line geometry and 122 features.

5. Select `Hawaii_Counties.shp` again and click on the Preview tab. This shows you the spatial features of this GIS dataset (shown in figure below).

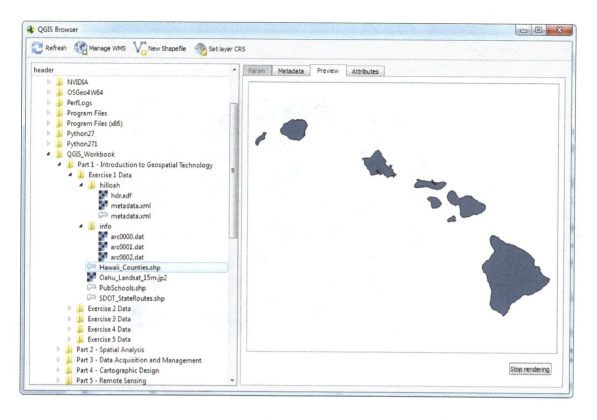

6. Click on the Attributes tab. This shows you the other component of the data model, the attributes. Each row corresponds to one polygon. The columns are things we know about the polygons such as island name (see figure below).

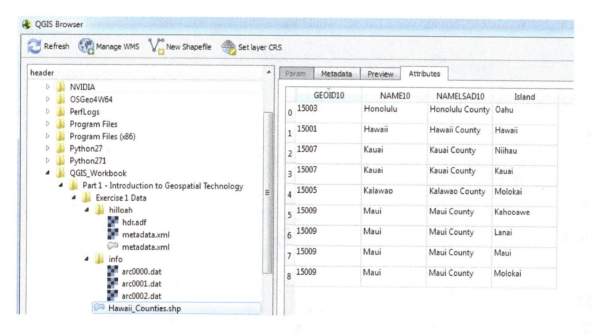

7. Select the `Oahu_Landsat_15m.jp2` dataset. Click on the Preview tab. This is an example of a raster dataset. Like a photograph, it is composed of cells. This raster is a satellite image of the island of Oahu, Hawaii (shown in figure below).

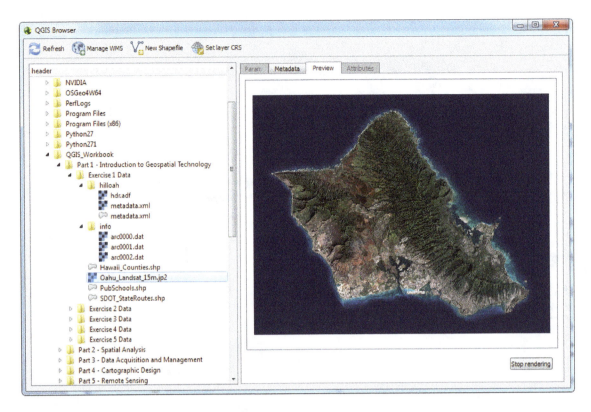

Let's look at the file formats in more detail.

8. Select the `Exercise 1 Data` folder in the File Tree. The `Param` tab is all that is available when a folder is selected (see figure below).

9. Now the Display Window is showing you what you would see in Windows Explorer.

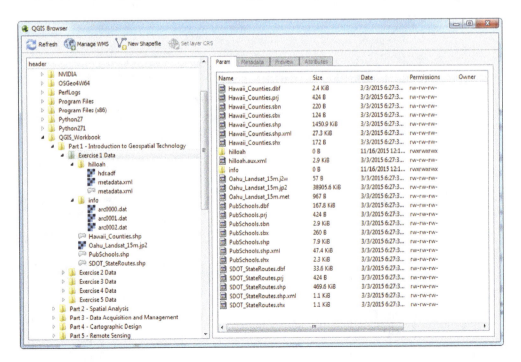

Focus on the Hawaii Counties files. Notice that the File Tree shows that Shapefile just as `Hawaii_Counties.shp` whereas the Display Window is showing seven files named Hawaii_Counties. These are all the component files of this particular shapefile. The File Tree simplifies the view of your data showing you only the *.shp* file.

For more information on ESRI shapefiles refer to this link

http://en.wikipedia.org/wiki/Shapefile

1.5   Task 3 - Viewing Geospatial Data in QGIS Desktop

Now that you know how geospatial datasets are stored on your computer, let's see what the data they contain look like. This next section will introduce you to QGIS Desktop.

1. Click Start | All Programs | QGIS | QGIS Desktop.

2. QGIS Desktop is the application you will use for making maps, editing data, and doing GIS analysis, among many other operations. QGIS Desktop has two main sections: the Layers panel and the Map Window.

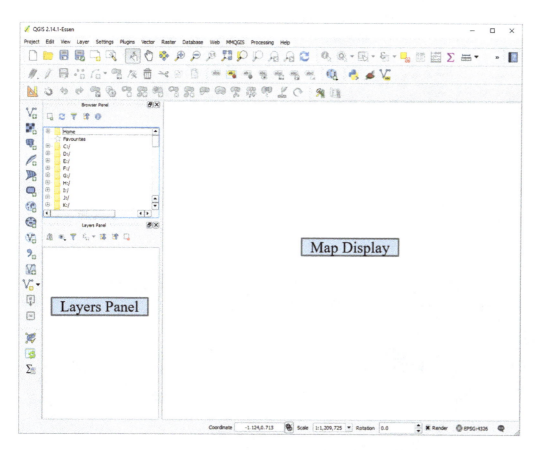

Note: Your QGIS Desktop window may look slightly different than the one pictured above. To reset your display back to the default settings, click the Settings | Options | System tab | QSettings section | Reset button, then click OK and restart QGIS Desktop.

The QGIS Desktop interface is a little cluttered by default, so let's close a few panels so we just see the Layers panel and Map Window.

3. Locate the Browser panel, and click the small 'X' button in the upper-right corner to close the panel (see

figure below).

4. Close the Shortest path panel using the same method.

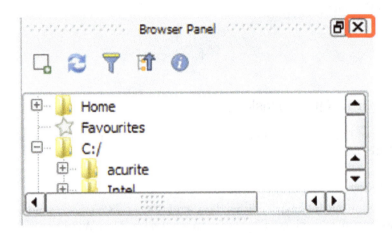

Panels can be docked and undocked from the QGIS Desktop window. To undock a panel, click and drag the panel's top title bar (outlined in figure below) and drag it away from the sides. When you release your mouse button, the panel will be floating freely.

To dock a floating panel, click and drag the title bar, and drag the panel to the left or right side of QGIS Desktop until a rectangle appears underneath the panel. Release the mouse button to dock the panel (docking action shown in figure below).

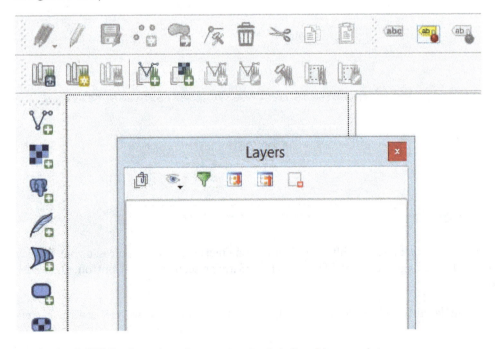

With the QGIS Desktop interface customized, let's add some data.

QGIS has Add Data buttons for each major geospatial data model (vector and raster).

5. Click the **Add Vector Layer** button 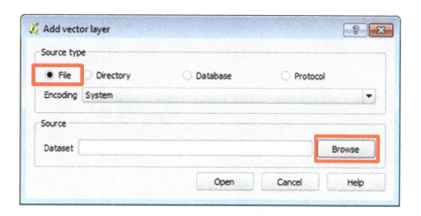. It's located on the toolbar along the left hand side of the Layers panel.

   - Alternatively, you can click Layer | Add Layer | Add Vector Layer.

6. This opens the **Add vector layer** window. Let's add one of the ESRI shapefiles which is a file-based dataset.

7. Keep the **Source type** "File" which is the default. Then click the **Browse** button.

Add vector layer	? ✕

Source type

● File   ○ Directory   ○ Database   ○ Protocol

Encoding System ▾

Source

Dataset [   ] Browse

Open   Cancel   Help

8. The **Open an OGR Supported Vector Layer** window opens. (NOTE: OGR is a FOSS4G project with the sole purpose to read and write geospatial vector data files.) The window defaults to all files. From exploring the exercise data in QGIS Browser, you know there are several shapefiles in the exercise data folder. Take a moment to see the other available options. Click the All files dropdown box and change to ESRI Shapefiles (shown in figure below).

All files (*)
GDAL/OGR VSIFileHandler (*.zip *.gz *.tar *.tar.gz *.tgz *
Arc/Info ASCII Coverage (*.e00 *.E00)
Atlas BNA (*.bna *.BNA)
AutoCAD DXF (*.dxf *.DXF)
Comma Separated Value (*.csv *.CSV)
ESRI Personal GeoDatabase (*.mdb *.MDB)
ESRI Shapefiles (*.shp *.SHP)
GPS eXchange Format [GPX] (*.gpx *.GPX)
Generic Mapping Tools [GMT] (*.gmt *.GMT)
GeoJSON (*.geojson *.GEOJSON)
GeoPackage (*.gpkg *.GPKG)
GeoRSS (*.xml *.XML)
Geoconcept (*.gxt *.txt *.GXT *.TXT)
Geographic Markup Language [GML] (*.xml *.GML)

9. Once you are finished exploring, make sure it is still set to ESRI Shapefiles. This filters what you can see in the exercise folder so that you only see the shapefiles.

10. Select `Hawaii_Counties.shp` and click Open (see figure below).

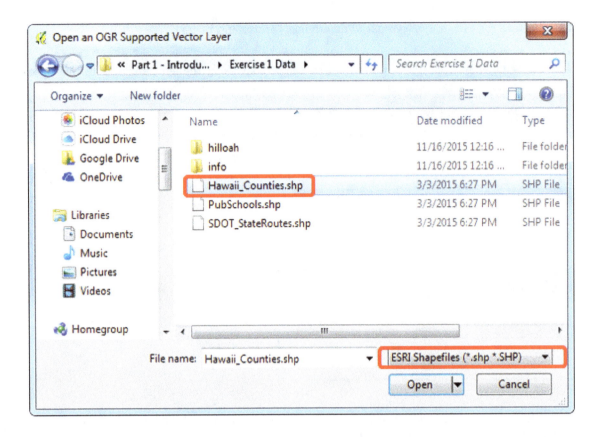

11. Now back at the Add vector layer window, click Open to add the data to QGIS Desktop (see figure below).

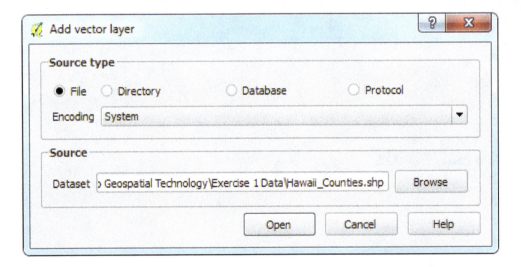

12. You will now see Hawaii_Counties in the Layers panel and the map features displayed in the map window. Vector GIS layers will come in with random colors. You will learn how to change layer styling in a future exercise.

13. Let's examine the attributes. Right-click on the Hawaii Counties layer in the Layers panel. This opens a context menu. Select Open Attribute Table (shown in figure below).

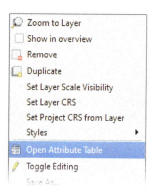

14. The attribute table opens. If you recall from exploring this dataset with QGIS Browser, it has 9 features (9 polygons). The attribute table has 9 corresponding records. There are columns with the County name (NAMELSAD10) and with the Island name (Island). Close the Attribute Table by clicking the X button in the upper right hand corner.

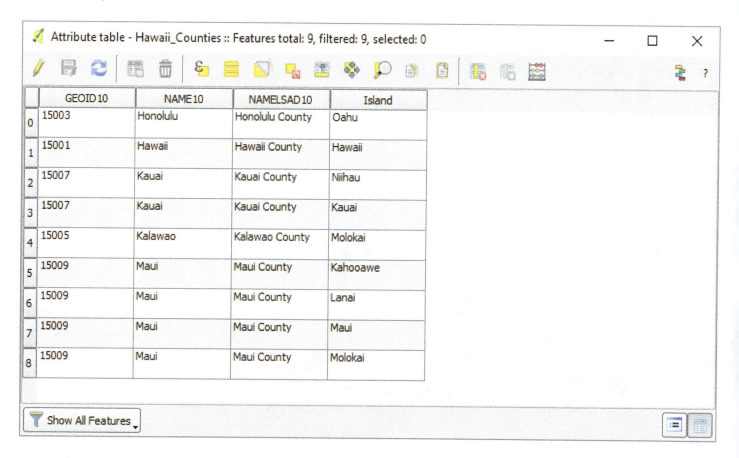

15. Another way to interact with both the spatial features and the attributes is the Identify button.

16. Click the Identify button

17. Click on one of the features on the map. The Identify Results panel (shown in figure below) shows you the attributes for the feature you clicked on. *Note:* The Identify Results panel may initially be docked or floating.

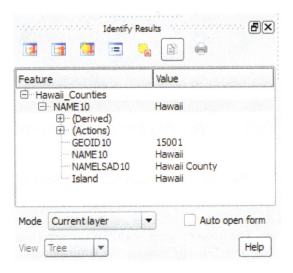

Now you will learn how to add Raster data to QGIS Desktop.

18. Click the **Add Raster Layer** button .

   • Alternatively, click Layer | Add Layer | Add Raster Layer.

19. The **Open a GDAL Supported Raster Data Source** window opens (displayed in figure below). This is a very similar workflow to adding vector data.

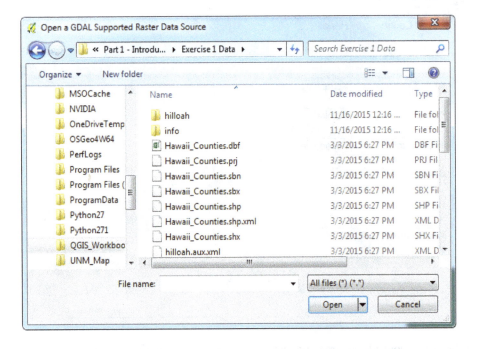

20. Whereas QGIS used OGR to open vector data files, here it uses another FOSS4G software library called GDAL. GDAL is used for reading and writing raster datasets.

21. The window's raster data filter is set to **All Files** by default, so you see the entire contents of the folder (Figure below).

22. Set the filter to ERDAS JPEG2000. (Also, note how many formats it will read!) In GIS there are many more raster file types than vector. Once you've set the filter you'll see the one dataset: `Oahu_Landsat_15m.jp2` (shown in figure below).

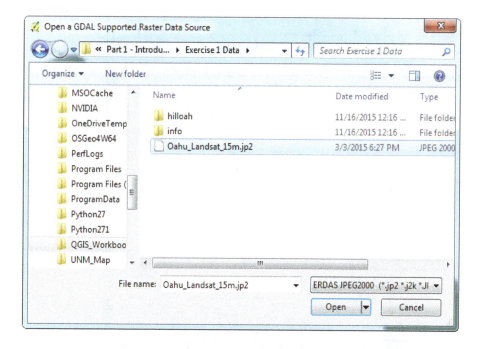

23. Select the `Oahu_Landsat_15m.jp2` raster dataset and click Open.

24. This dataset only covers a portion of Hawaii—just the island of Oahu. Right-click on the Oahu_Landsat_15m dataset in the layers panel and choose **Zoom to Layer** to zoom to the spatial extent of this raster (shown in figure below).

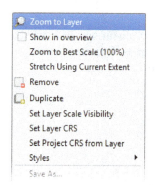

You may notice two folders in the exercise data folder that we have not discussed yet. One is named `hilloah` and the other `info`. Together, these combine to make another geospatial raster dataset format named GRID. The info folder holds the attributes and always has the name "info". The other folder is the layer name and contains the spatial data. Let's add a GRID raster to our map.

25. Click the **Add Raster Layer** button again.

26. Set the filter to Arc/Info Binary Grid. Double click the `hilloah` folder to enter it. Select the `hdr.adf` file and click Open to add the raster to QGIS (shown in figure below).

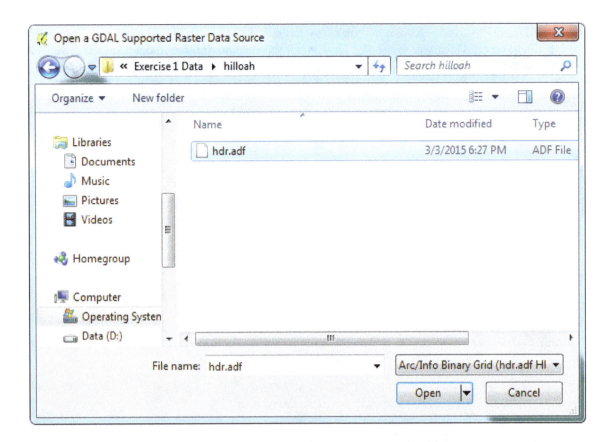

27. This raster is a hillshade image of Oahu and it represents the terrain.

QGIS Desktop also has a Browser panel that allows us to view geospatial files on our computer without having to open QGIS Browser.

28. Right-click on the blank space to the right of the Help menu. This opens a context menu showing all the toolbars and windows that you can add to the QGIS interface. Check the box next to **Browser** (shown in figure below). A Browser panel is added to QGIS Desktop (likely located under the Layers panel).

29. Look at the Browser panel. Note that there is a **Favourites** item. Identify folders or locations as being favorites in order for them to appear here.

Data is often stored deep inside a series of folders. It is often tedious and time consuming to navigate deep inside the folders to gain access to the data. Favorites provide a way to create a shortcut directly to any folder so that you have one-click access. Let's create a favorite to our exercise folder for practice.

30. Navigate to the `Exercise 1 Data` folder in the Browser panel. Right-click on it and choose Add as a Favourite (see figure below). *Note:* Currently this functionality is reserved only for the Browser tab in QGIS Desktop. However, once it is set it will show up as a favorite in QGIS Browser as well.

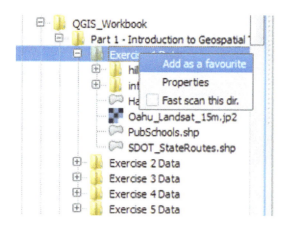

31. Now expand Favourites and you will see your exercise folder listed there. You can remove a favorite anytime by right-clicking on it and choosing Remove favourite.

32. Expand the exercise folder under Favourites to expose the contents. Select `SDOT_StateRoutes.shp` and drag it onto the map. This is a quick way to add data to your map.

Note: You can drag data from the QGIS Browser application to QGIS Desktop as well to add the data to the map.

1.6 Conclusion

In this exercise you explored datasets that use the two common geospatial data models: vector and raster. You have also used the QGIS Browser to preview datasets. In future exercises, you will learn how to use QGIS Desktop to make maps and perform analysis.

1.7 Discussion Questions

1. How can Browser favourites make your workflow more efficient?

2. What are the two main parts of a GIS data model?

3. Name three ways of seeing feature attributes for a vector GIS layer.

Exercise 2

Displaying Geospatial Data

Objective – Explore and Understand How to Display Geospatial Data

2.1 Introduction

In this exercise, you'll learn how to complete a well-designed map showing the relationship between species habitat and federal land ownership, as well as how to style GIS data layers in QGIS Desktop. In addition, we'll show how to use the QGIS Print Composer to design a well crafted map deliverable. The final map will include standard map elements such as the title and map legend.

This exercise will also continue to introduce you to the QGIS interface, as QGIS Desktop will be used throughout the course. It is important to learn the concepts in this exercise as future exercises will require the skills covered in this exercise.

This exercise includes the following tasks:

- Task 1 – Add data, organize map layers and set map projections.
- Task 2 – Style data layers.
- Task 3 – Compose map deliverable.

2.2 Objective: Create a Map that Meets the Customer's Requirements

Often times, you will be provided with a map requirements document from a coworker or customer. For this exercise, the you'll respond to a map requirements document from a customer who is writing a paper about the state of Greater sage-grouse habitat in the western United States. The map requirements from the customer are below.

Map Requirements from Customer:

Hi, my name is Steve Darwin. I am a wildlife biologist writing a paper on the state of Greater sage-grouse (see figure below) populations in the western United States. I need a letter sized, color, map figure that shows the relationship between current occupied Greater sage-grouse habitat and federal land ownership. I am interested in seeing how much habitat is under federal versus non-federal ownership.

I have been provided data from the US Fish and Wildlife Service depicting current occupied range for Greater sage-grouse. I also have federal land ownership, state boundaries and country boundaries from the US National Atlas. The land ownership data has an attribute column describing which federal agency manages the land (AGBUR).

I want to have the habitat data shown so that the federal land ownership data is visible beneath. I would like each different type of federal land styled with standard Bureau of Land Management colors. The map should also

29

include a title ("Greater sage-grouse Current Distribution"), a legend, data sources and the date. The map should be a high-resolution (300 dpi) jpg image.

I trust that you will get the figure right the first time, so please just submit the completed figures to the managing editor directly.

Image attribution: By Pacific Southwest Region from Sacramento, US (Greater Sage-Grouse) [CC BY 2.0 (http: //creativecommons.org/licenses/by/2.0)], via Wikimedia Commons.

2.3   Task 1 - Add Data, Organize Map Layers and Set Coordinate Reference System

In this first task you will learn a new way to add data to QGIS Desktop. You will then set the projection for the map project, organize the data layers in the Table of Contents and change the layer names.

1. Open QGIS Desktop.

In Exercise 1 you learned how to add data to QGIS Desktop by using the Add Vector Data and Add Raster Data buttons. Now you will learn another method of adding data to QGIS Desktop. You will use the QGIS Desktop Browser panel.

2. Click View | Panels and make sure Browser is checked. The Browser panel will now be displayed.

Note: The Browser panel may be docked or floating, so it may not be in the same location as in the figures in this exercise.

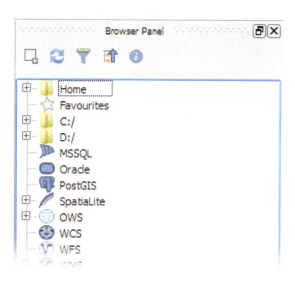

3. Using the file tree in the Browser window navigate to the **Exercise 2 Data** folder.

4. Right click on the **Exercise 2 Data** folder and choose **Add as a favourite** from the context menu.

5. Sometimes when recent changes have been made, such as setting a folder as a favourite, the Refresh button needs to be pressed in order to see the changes. Click the **Refresh** button (highlighted in figure below).

6. Now expand Favourites near the top of the file tree in the Browser window by clicking the plus sign to the left. You will see the **Exercise 2 Data** folder listed. Setting the folder as a favorite allows you to quickly navigate to your working folder.

7. You will see 5 shapefiles in the exercise data folder:

   - Canada.shp
   - Land_ownership.shp
   - Mexico.shp
   - Sage_grouse_current_distribution.shp
   - Western_states.shp

8. You can select them all by holding down the Ctrl key on your keyboard while left clicking on each shapefile. Select the five shapefiles (shown in figure below).

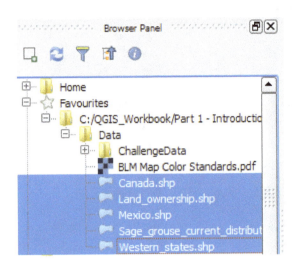

9. Drag the five selected shapefiles onto the map canvas from the Browser panel. This is another way of adding geospatial data to QGIS Desktop. QGIS Desktop should now look like figure below. The random colors that QGIS assigns to the layers may be different than the figure below but that is fine.

   - *Note:* If you do not see anything displayed in the map canvas, you may need to zoom to full extents of the map by pressing the Zoom Full button 🔍. Alternatively, you can click View | Zoom Full.

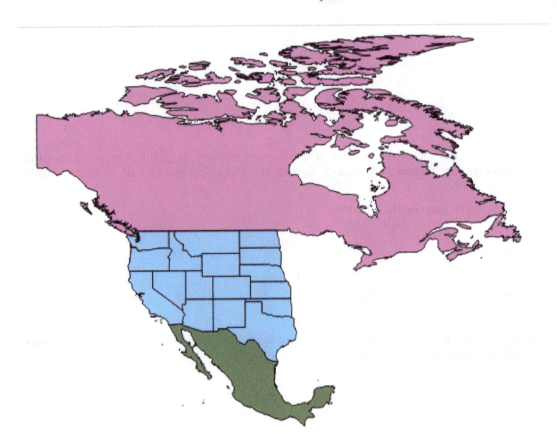

10. Let's save the QGIS project. Click on Project | Save from the menu bar. Navigate to your **Exercise 2 Data** folder and save your project as **Exercise 2**.

11. You have five layers in the map canvas, but currently all you can see are data for Canada, Mexico and the Western states. When you cannot see a dataset, one approach is to make sure the spatial extent of your map

window covers that dataset. Right click on the Sage_grouse_current_distribution layer in the Layers panel, and choose **Zoom to Layer** from the context menu. This will zoom you into the extent of that dataset.

12. The map is now zoomed to the western United States, but we still cannot see anything that looks like habitat data (shown in figure below).

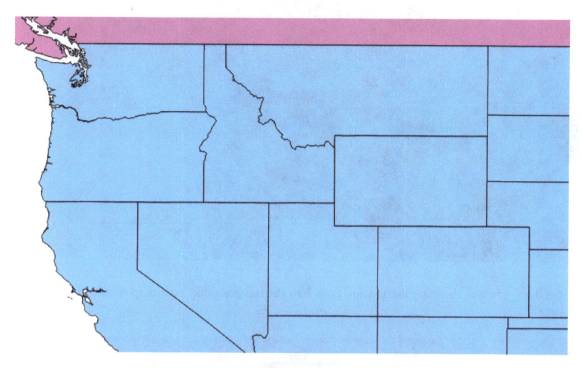

The data layers in the Layers panel are drawn in the order they appear in. So the layer that is on the top of the list in the Layers panel will be drawn on top of the other layers in the map view. Notice that the Western_states layer is in that top position. This mean that Western_states is covering up the Sage_grouse_current_distribution and Land_ownership data, since they are placed lower in the Layers panel.

Let's change this drawing order.

13. Select the Land_ownership data layer in the Layers panel and drag it to the top position. You will see a blue line as you drag this layer up the list.

14. Your map should now resemble the figure below.

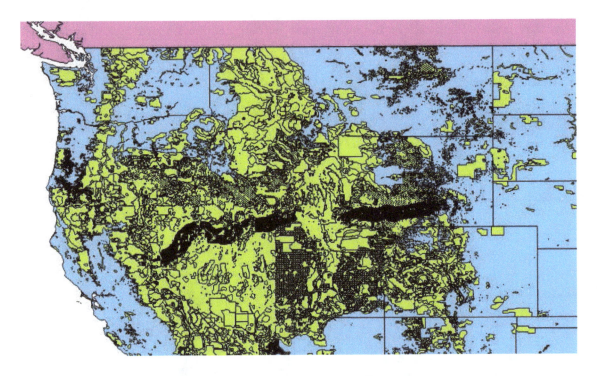

15. Now drag the Sage_grouse_current_distribution layer into the top position. Your map should now resemble the figure below.

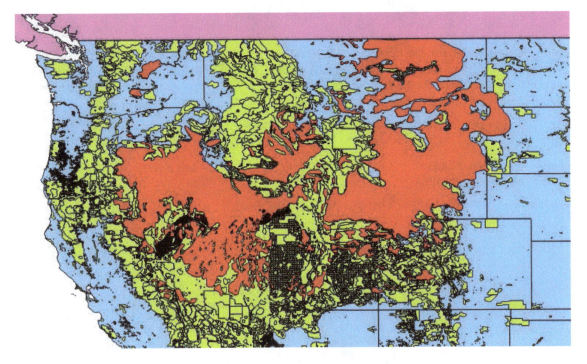

Now all the data layers should be in the correct order. Typically, data layers will be organized with point data layers on top of line layers on top of polygon layers. Raster data layers are usually placed near the bottom.

With the layers in the best drawing order, let's turn our attention to the coordinate reference system for the map.

16. Note that the lower right hand corner of QGIS displays EPSG: 4269 OTF. This is the EPSG code for the coordinate reference system (CRS) the map is currently in and an indication that on-the-fly projection is

enabled (shown in figure below).

17. Click on Project | Project Properties from the menu bar to open the Project Properties window.

18. Select the CRS tab.

The current QGIS map CRS is listed at the bottom. This is a detailed explanation of the maps CRS which is a geographic coordinate system using the NAD83 datum. This CRS makes the lower 48 look stretched out and distorted, so you'll want to change the maps CRS into something that makes the lower 48 "look correct".

19. Make sure that the Enable 'on the fly' CRS transformation option is checked. Click OK to close the Project Properties window.

Since the Sage_grouse_current_distribution layer is in an Albers projection, and the QGIS map is in a geographic CRS, that means that the Sage_grouse_current_distribution layer is being projected on the fly into the geographic projection of the map.

20. Right click on the Sage_grouse_current_distribution layer and choose Set Project CRS from Layer option on the context menu (Figure below). This will put the map into the Albers CRS of the Sage grouse layer. Note that the EPSG code in the lower right corner now reads 5070 for the Albers CRS. This CRS gives the western US an appearance we are more used to. Any other map layers not in Albers, will now be projected on the fly into Albers.

Now you will change the layer names in the Layers panel. The layer names match the names of the shapefiles by default. However, these names will appear on the legend. So you will always want to change these to proper names that your map reading audience will understand.

21. Right click on the Sage_grouse_current_distribution layer, and choose the Properties from the context menu, to open the Layer Properties window. Choose the General tab on the left. Click in the box next to Layer name and change the name to Sage-grouse Habitat (shown in figure below). Click OK to close the Layer Properties window.

   • Alternatively, you can right click on a layer in the Layers panel and choose Rename from the context menu to make the layer name editable directly in the Layers panel.

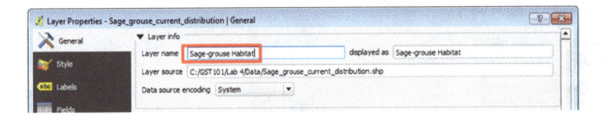

22. Change the other layers names as follows:
    - Change Land ownership to Federal Land Ownership
    - Change Western_states to State Boundaries
23. Click the File | Save to save the changes you have made to your project.

2.4 Task 2 - Style Data Layers

Now that you have set up your map, you will style your layers and begin to craft a well-designed map.

Visually you will want the land ownership and sage-grouse habitat to have the most weight. Canada and Mexico are there for reference but should fall to the background. You will make them both light gray.

1. Double-click on the Canada layer to open the Layer Properties window (this is another way to open Layer Properties).
2. Click on the Style tab.
3. In the Symbol layers box click on Simple fill (reference figure below).

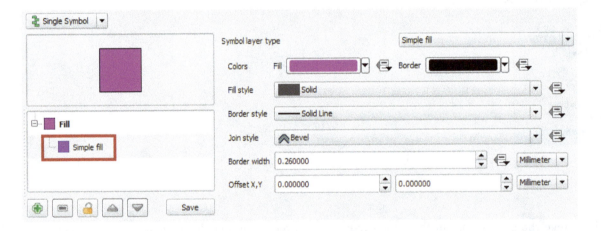

4. Find the Symbol layer type box on the right side of the window. This allows you to change both the fill and outline symbols for this polygon layer. Click on the colored box to the right of Fill (shown in figure below) to open the Color picker window.

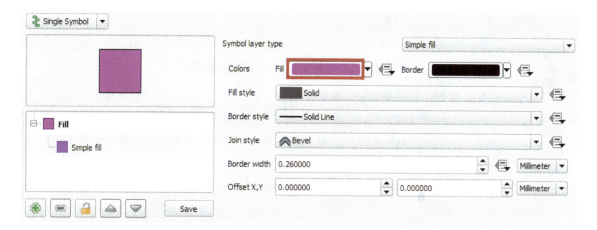

You can pick existing Basic colors or define a color via A) hue, saturation and value (HSV) or B) red blue and green (RGB) values. Set the color to Hue: 0 Sat: 0% and Val: 90%. Make sure your Color picker window matches the figure below.

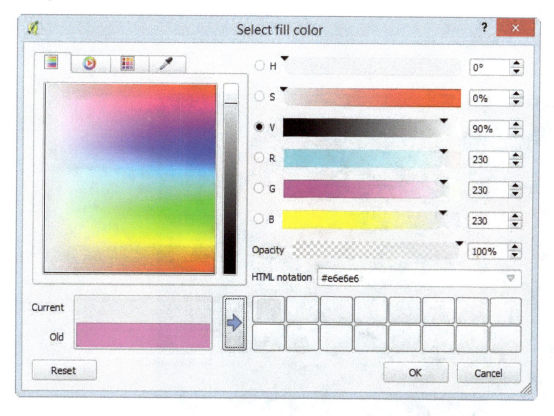

5. Click the button with the blue arrow to add the color to the custom color buttons. Click OK to close the Color picker window.

6. Back in the Layer Properties window, for the **Border style**, select Solid Line from the dropdown menu (shown in figure below).

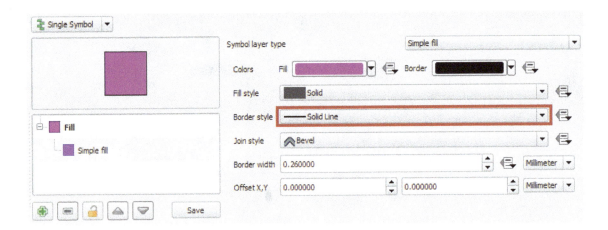

7. Click OK on the Layer Properties window to close and style the Canada layer.

8. Open Layer Properties for Mexico. Make Mexico look the same as Canada. You can just choose the Custom color you just saved to save time.

Your map should now look like figure below.

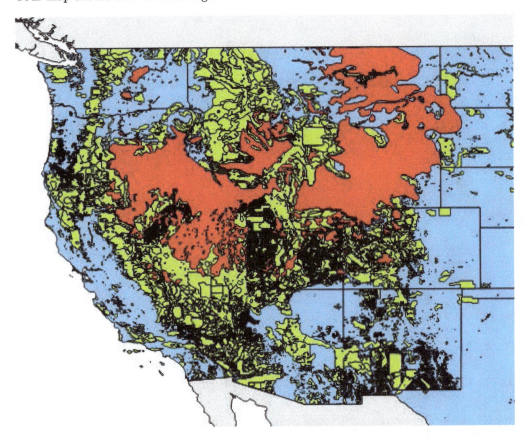

9. Using the same workflow, give the State Boundaries a white fill. You will be able to find white in the Basic colors palette.

Now you will style the Land Ownership layer. Instead of making the entire layer one color as you have done thus far, you will assign a unique color to each land managing agency. How do you know who is managing each parcel? This will be information contained in the attribute table.

10. Right click on Federal Land Ownership layer in the Layers panel, and choose Open the Attribute Table from the context menu.

There are thirteen columns of information. Can you find the one that contains the land manager?

11. Open the Layer Properties for the Federal Land Ownership layer and switch to the Style tab. So far you've used the default Single Symbol type. Now you will switch to Categorized.

12. Click the drop down menu and change from Single Symbol to Categorized (Figure below).

Now you have the option of choosing an attribute column to symbolize the layer by. The column AGBUR is the one that contains the managing agency values.

13. Click the drop down arrow and choose AGBUR for the Column.

14. Click the Classify button (shown in figure below). This tells QGIS to sort through all the records in the table and identify all the unique values. Now you can assign a specific color to each class by double clicking on the color square.

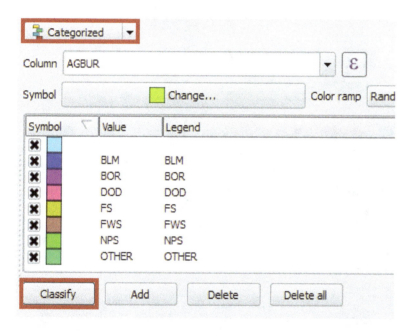

Notice that there is a symbol with no values. These are parcels with no values (NULL) in the AGBUR field. They represent private and state inholdings within federal lands. Since you are just interested in depicting federal land ownership you'll delete that symbol class.

15. Select that top symbol by clicking on it, and then click the Delete button below to remove that symbol. Now those parcels will not be included on the map.

For the remaining federal land ownership symbols you will use the BLM Standards Manual for land ownership maps http://www.blm.gov/noc/st/en/business/mapstandards/colormod.html.

- *Note:* A PDF of the BLM Map Color Standards is also available in your exercise folder and is named BLM Map Color Standards.pdf.

The BLM has designated colors for each type of land ownership. When composing a map it is important to pay attention to industry specific standards. Following them will make the map more intuitive to the target audience.

For example, people are used to seeing Forest Service land depicted in a certain shade of green.

16. To color BLM lands, double click on the color patch left of BLM in the Style window. The Symbol selector will open.

17. Click on **Simple fill**.

18. You will not want any border lines on these polygons. With such a complicated thematic polygon layer they are too visually distracting. Choose a **Border style** of **No Pen**.

19. Click on the **Fill style** color patch to open the Color Picker window.

20. In the Color Picker window, change the Red, Green, and Blue values to 254, 230, and 121 respectively (shown in figure below). This will change the color to a specific shade of tan representing BLM lands. Click OK in the Color Picker window. Then click OK in the Symbol Selector to save the BLM style.

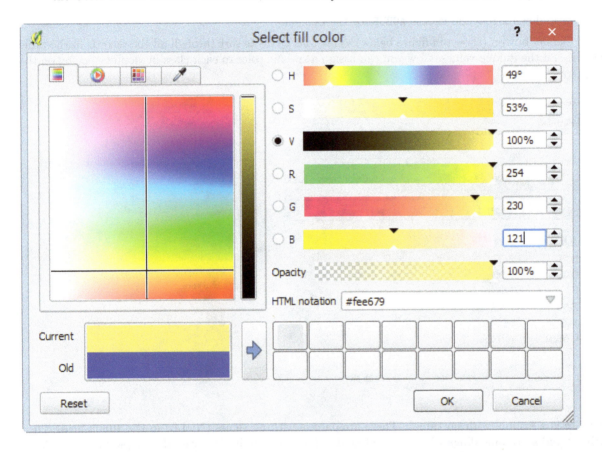

21. Use the values below to change the RGB colors for the remaining six land ownership classes. Also choose **No pen** for the border style.

   - BOR – 255, 255, 179
   - DOD – 251, 180, 206
   - FS – 179, 222, 105
   - FWS – 127, 204, 167
   - NPS – 177, 137, 193
   - OTHER – 150, 150, 150

22. When finished, click OK on the Layer Properties for Federal Land Ownership.

23. Turn off Sage-grouse Habitat by clicking the X next to the name in the Layers panel.

Your map should now resemble figure below.

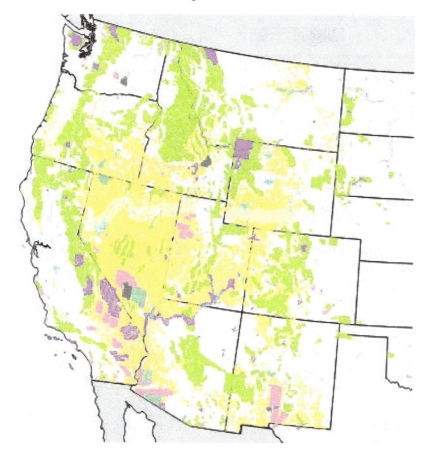

Now you will set a background color for the map. Since states are filled with white, setting a background color of light blue will serve to represent the Pacific Ocean.

24. From the menu bar choose Project | Project Properties.

25. On the General tab, click the white color patch next to Background color to open the Color Picker window.

26. Set the RGB value to: 225, 255, 255.

27. Click OK on the Color Picker window and OK on Project Properties to save the setting.

Depending on your current map extent, the area east of the states layer may be blue now too. That is fine. For the final map we will be zoomed in so you won't see that.

The states are white with a black border and serve to show non-federal land as white which is great. However, the state boundaries are obscured since State Boundaries are below Federal Land Ownership.

28. Go to the Browser panel and add Western_states.shp to the map again. You can have multiple copies of layers for cartographic purposes.

29. Drag the Western_states layer to the top of the Layers panel.

30. Open the Layer Properties window for the Western_states layer and select the Style tab.

31. Click on Simple fill.

32. Give the layer a Fill style of No Brush (see figure below). It will now just be the state outlines above Federal Land Ownership.

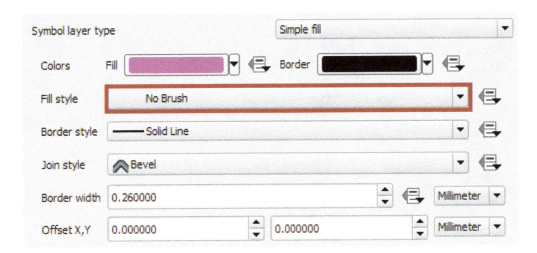

33. Click OK to save the style and close the Layer Properties window.

34. Your map should now resemble figure below.

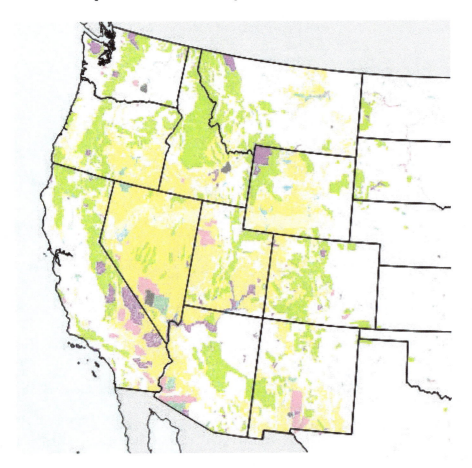

The last layer to work with is the Sage-grouse Habitat. You will make the Sage-grouse Habitat polygons have a crosshatch pattern. This will allow the map reader to see the land ownership data beneath.

35. Turn on the visibility for the Sage-grouse Habitat layer.

36. Open the Layer Properties for Sage-grouse Habitat.

37. Click on Simple fill.

38. Change the Fill color to RGB 170, 0, 255.

39. Change the Border color to RGB 142, 0, 213.

40. Make the Fill style FDiagonal.

41. Finally change the Border width to 0.46 (reference settings in figure below).

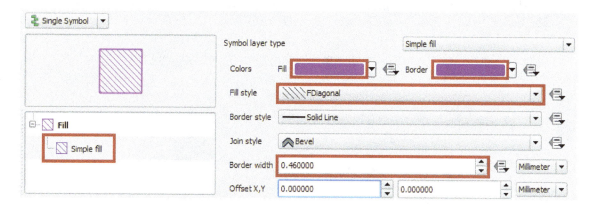

42. Click OK.

43. Save your project!

Your map should now resemble the figure below.

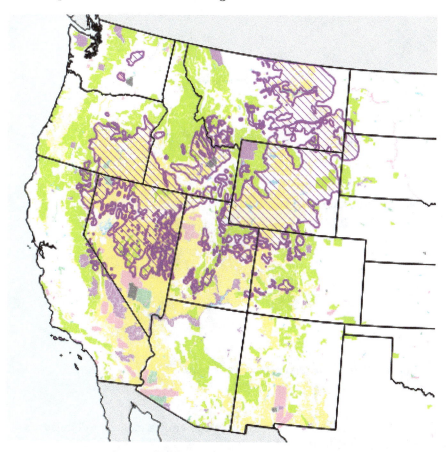

2.5   Task 3 - Compose Map Deliverable

Now that all the data is well styled you can compose the map deliverable.

1. Zoom in tighter to the Sage-grouse Habitat data.

   - Use the Zoom in tool and drag a box encapsulating the sage-grouse habitat. Leave a little of the Pacific Ocean visible to the west to give some context (reference figure below).

As it turns out, the data for Mexico is not needed. Sometimes you are given data that does not end up being used, but is nice to have in case you do need it.

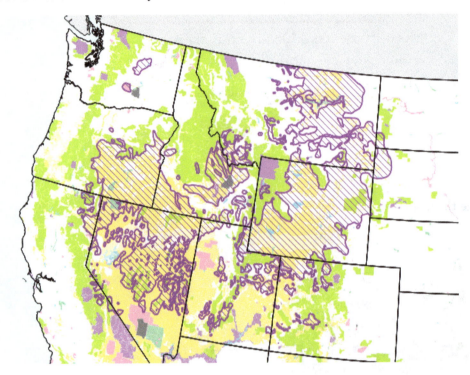

2. From the menu bar choose Project | New Print Composer.
3. Name the Composer "Exercise 2 - Sage-grouse Habitat" (shown in figure below).

4. Click OK. The Print Composer will open. This is where you craft your map.

The Print Composer is an application window with many tools that allow you to craft a map. For detailed information about the Print Composer, refer to the QGIS manual:
http://www.qgis.org/en/docs/user_manual/print_composer/print_composer.html
The main window of the Print Composer displays the piece of paper upon which the map will be designed. There

are buttons along the left side of the window that allow you to add various map elements: map, scale bar, photo, text, shapes, attribute tables, etc. Each item added to the map canvas becomes a graphic object that can be further manipulated (if selected) by the Items tab on the right side of the composer. Across the top are buttons for exporting the composition, navigating within the composition and some other graphic tools (grouping/ungrouping etc.)

5. On the Composition tab you can specify details about the overall composition. Set the Presets to ANSI A (Letter; 8.5x11 in).

6. Set the Orientation to Landscape.

7. Set the Export resolution to 300 DPI.

(These are listed as map requirements at the beginning of the exercise.)

8. Using the Add new map button ⬚ drag a box on the map canvas where you'd like the map to go. Remember that you'll need room for a title at the top of the page and a legend to the right of the map (reference figure below).

The map object can be resized after it's added by selecting it and using the handles around the perimeter to resize.

Map extent helpful hints: Generally, the map will look as it does within QGIS Desktop. However, you may need to change the map extent in QGIS Desktop, go back to the Print Composer and click the Refresh view button ↻. It is normal to have some back and forth with QGIS Desktop and the Print Composer before getting the map just right.

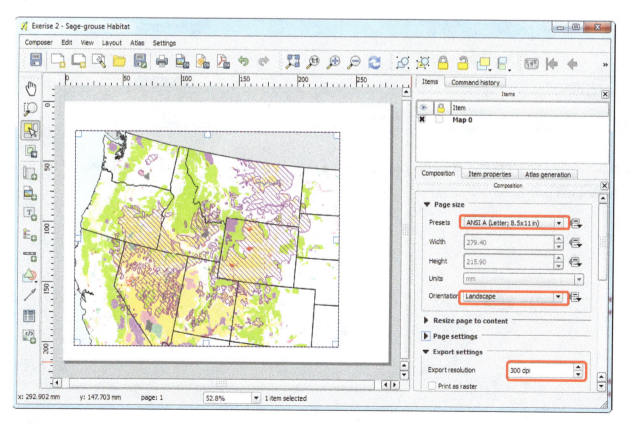

Now you will add the title to your map.

9. Use the Add new label tool 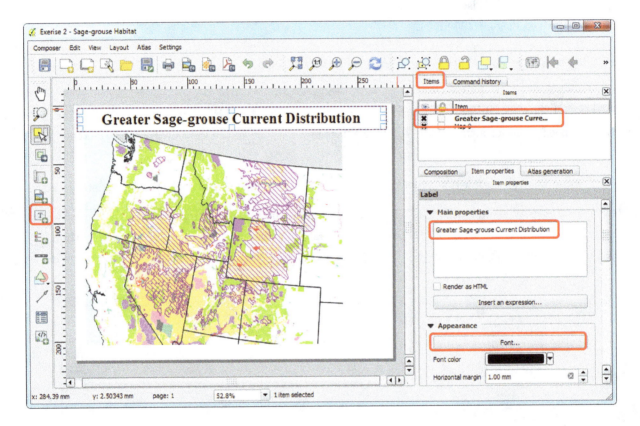 to drag a box all the way across the top of the composition. The text box can be resized after the fact by using the graphic handles.

10. Use the Item Properties to type in the title. Enter the title as 'Greater sage-grouse Current Distribution'.

11. In the Items tab, select the title. This will change the properties available in the Item Properties tab.

12. In the Item Properties tab, click the Font button and change the font to: Times New Roman, Bold, Size 36.

13. Finally align the title horizontally to the center of the map (see figure below).

14. Now you will add a legend. Use the Add new legend tool to drag a box on the right side of the map (shown in figure below).

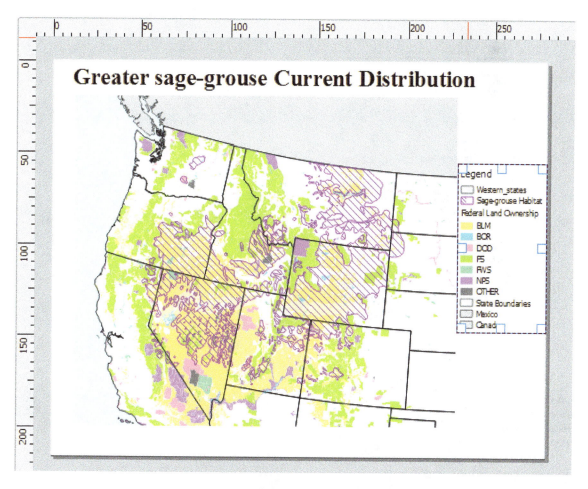

The upper most Western_states layer does not need to appear in the legend, nor does Mexico. Western_states is there purely for cartographic reasons and Mexico does not appear on the map. The Item properties tab will be used to configure the legend (see figure below).

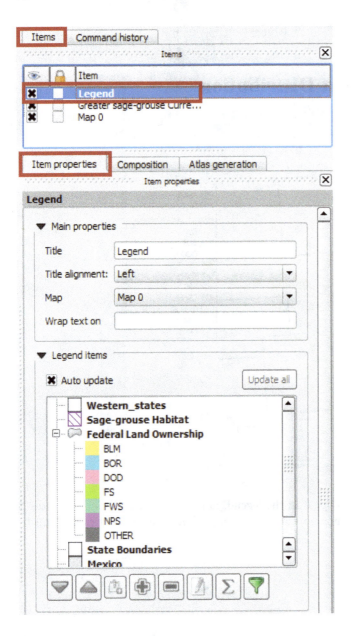

15. Uncheck Auto update. This will enable us to modify the legend, however, updates to the map will no longer be reflected in the legend unless we reenable Auto update.

16. Select the Western_states layer and click the Delete item button to remove it. Do the same for Mexico.

17. Expand the Federal Land Ownership layer.

18. Click on the BLM class and click the Edit button.

19. Change the name to "Bureau of Land Management". Go through each remaining land ownership class and edit them to match the figure below.

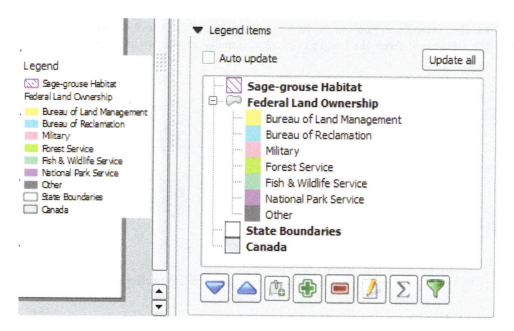

Now we will add a neatline around our map.

20. Click the tool (shown in figure below).

21. Drag a box around the map object and legend.
22. On the Item Properties tab, click the **Style Change** button.
23. Click **Simple fill** and give it a **Fill style** of **No Brush**.
24. Give it a **Border width** of 1.
25. Adjust the box so that it aligns with the map boundary.

You may find it necessary to lock the rectangle so you can move other map elements. To lock a map element and keep it from being selected, in the Items tab, check the box in the lock column as shown in the figure below.

The last items to add to the map are the data sources and date.

26. Click the Add new label tool.

27. Drag a box in the lower right hand corner of the composition. Using the Item Properties type:

Data Sources: The National Atlas & USFWS

Date: Month, Day, Year

28. Make the font Times New Roman and the font size 8.

Your map should resemble the figure below.

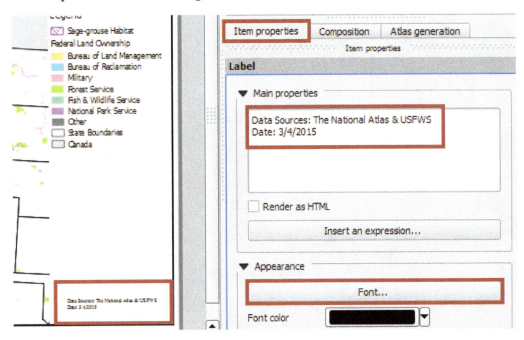

29. Congratulations your map is finished! The final step is to export it to a high-resolution jpg image.

30. Click the Export as image button 🖼️ .

31. Choose JPEG as the Save as type and save the image to your Exercise 2 Data folder. Name the file exercise2_Map.jpg and click Save.

32. The final map should look like the figure below.

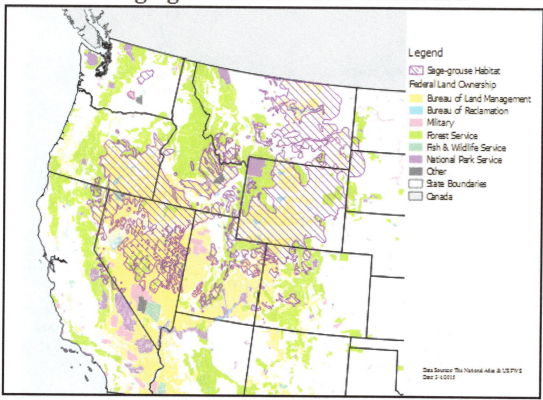

2.6 Conclusion

In this exercise you created a well-designed map using some of the cartography tools available in QGIS Desktop. You created a nice map highlighting federal land ownership within sage-grouse habitat for a client. This involved styling layers, styling layers by categorical attributes and crafting a map composition.

2.7 Discussion Questions

1. Export the final map as a high-resolution jpg for your instructor to grade.
2. What are two ways to add vector data to QGIS Desktop?
3. How would a portrait orientation change the composition of the map? Describe how you would arrange the map elements.
4. No map is perfect. Critique this map. What do you like about it? What do you dislike about it? How would you change this map to improve it? Would you add other data layers or add labels?

2.8 Challenge Assignment (optional)

Another biologist working with black bears on the east coast heard about your great work on the sage-grouse map. She would like you to create a similar map for her. The data she is providing is in the `Exercise 2 Data/Challenge` folder.

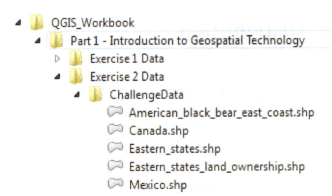

She also needs a letter sized, color, map figure that shows the relationship between black bear habitat and federal land ownership along the eastern seaboard. She is interested in seeing how much habitat is under federal versus non-federal ownership.

She is providing data from the US Fish and Wildlife Service depicting current occupied range for black bear on the east coast. She is also providing federal land ownership, state boundaries and country boundaries from the US National Atlas. The land ownership data has an attribute column describing which federal agency manages the land (AGBUR). This land ownership dataset has another category in the AGBUR field for Wilderness Areas called "Wild". These should be styled with a dark green.

She wants to have the habitat data shown so that the federal land ownership data is visible beneath. She would like each different type of federal land styled with standard Bureau of Land Management colors. The map should also include a title ("Black Bear Current Distribution"), a legend, data sources and the date. The map should be a high-resolution (300 dpi) jpg image. Perhaps you can incorporate some improvements to this map!

Exercise 3

Creating Geospatial Data

Objective – Digitize Information from a Scanned Hardcopy Source

3.1 Introduction

In this exercise, you'll learn how to georeference a scanned map. Georeferencing is the process of transforming the coordinate system of the scanned map, from the coordinate system produced by the scanning process, into a real world projected coordinate reference system. You'll then learn how to digitize information contained in the scanned map into a shapefile. The first task will be to create the empty shapefile to digitize features into. In addition, you'll learn how to edit existing vector datasets.

This exercise will continue to introduce you to the QGIS interface. It is important to learn the concepts in this exercise, as later exercises in this workbook will require the skills covered here.

This exercise includes the following tasks:

- Task 1 – Create a new shapefile.

- Task 2 – Transforming coordinate system of source data.

- Task 3 – Heads-up digitizing from transformed source data.

- Task 4 – Editing existing geospatial data.

3.2 Objective: Digitize Information from a Scanned Hard Copy Source

While there is a large amount of digital information readily available to users of GIS, there's still a large amount of information that has not been converted to digital format. For hundreds of years of hard copy paper maps contained all geospatial data. Many historic, and even newer, hard copy maps have never been digitized. It is possible to extract the information from hardcopy sources through a process called digitizing. In this exercise, you will use heads-up digitizing to digitize parcels in a portion of Albuquerque, New Mexico from a scanned map. This will be accomplished through a five-step digitizing process:

1. Create a shapefile to store the data that will be digitized.
2. Load the scanned map source data into QGIS
3. Georeference the source map
4. Digitize parcels
5. Save

3.3   Task 1 - Create a New Shapefile

In Task 3, you will be digitizing parcels from a georeferenced data source. In this first task you will learn how to create the new shapefile you will eventually digitize into.

1. Open QGIS Browser.

2. Navigate to the exercise folder in the file tree and select the **Data** folder by clicking once on it so that it is highlighted.

3. Click on the **New Shapefile** button at the top of the Browser window. This will open the **New Shapefile Layer** window.

 New Shapefile

4. Choose a type of 'Polygon'

5. Click the Select CRS button to open the Coordinate Reference System Selector.

The City of Albuquerque, like most American municipalities, uses the State Plane Coordinate System (SPCS) for their data. You will use the same CRS for your new shapefile.

6. In the Coordinate Reference System Selector interface type New Mexico into the Filter. This will limit the list below to just those with New Mexico in their name. These are different SPCS CRSs for New Mexico. New Mexico has 3 zones and Albuquerque is in the Central zone.

7. Select the NAD83(HARN) / New Mexico Central (ftUS) with an EPSG code of 2903 (see figure below). Click OK once you have selected this CRS to be returned to the **New Shapefile Layer** window.

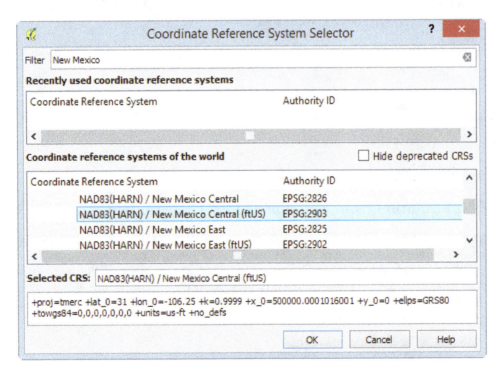

While creating your new shapefile you have the option of adding attribute columns. It is possible to add them later, but if you know of some attribute columns you will need in the layer, it makes the most sense to define them here. The ID attribute is automatically added to every shapefile you create.

For this exercise, you will need an attribute column to hold the zoning code.

8. In the New field section of the New Shapefile Layer window, define a new field named `zonecode` as Text data with a width of 5.

This means the new `zonecode` attribute column will store data as text and will only be able to accommodate five characters of data. Since our longest zoning code is 4 digits this is more than enough.

9. Click Add to fields list and you will see the new `zonecode` attribute added.

10. Click OK to approve the new shapefile options and open the Save layer as... window. Since you had the Data folder selected when you clicked the New Shapefile button it will default to that folder. If it doesn't just navigate to that folder now.

11. Name the shapefile `parcels.shp` and click Save to create the shapefile

Initially, the new shapefile may not display in the Browser. We need to first refresh the view to see the newly created file.

12. Click the Refresh button in the upper left hand corner of the QGIS Browser window. Expand the Data folder and you will see the `parcels.shp` file.

13. Select the `parcels.shp` dataset and click the Metadata tab. You'll see that it has 0 features and has the Spatial Reference System you specified. The New Mexico Central State Plane zone uses the Mercator projection since it is a north–south oriented zone.

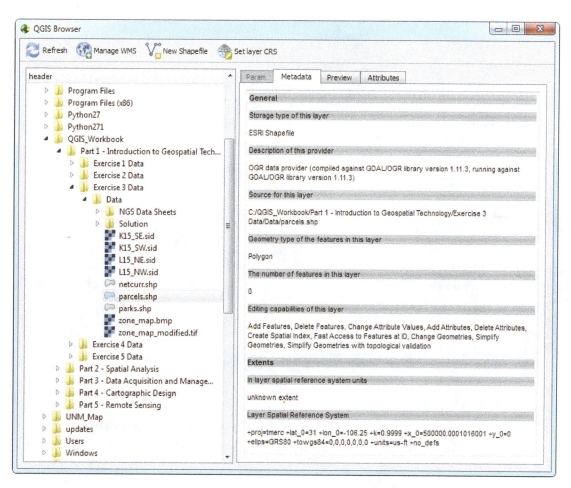

3.4   Task 2 - Transforming Coordinate System of Source Data

Now that you have created an empty shapefile to store the digitized information, you will perform a coordinate transformation (also known as georeferencing) on the source data set so that it is in an Earth-based coordinate system. In this case, the coordinate system will match your parcel shapefile (NAD83(HARN) / New Mexico Central (ftUS)).

To perform this task you will be using a plugin. Plugins are small add-ons to QGIS. Some are created by the core QGIS development team and others are created by third party developers.

1. Open QGIS Desktop.

2. Open QGIS Browser.

3. Arrange Browser and Desktop so that you can see both windows simultaneously on your desktop.

4. In Browser find the new parcels shapefile. Select it and drag it onto the map window of QGIS Desktop. This is another way to add data to Desktop.

5. From the Menu bar in QGIS Desktop, choose Project | Project Properties.

6. Click the CRS tab and Enable 'on the fly' CRS transformation. Click OK to save the setting and close the properties window.

7. The project should now have a CRS of EPSG 2903 (which is NAD83(HARN) / New Mexico Central (ftUS)) and on the fly CRS transformation is enabled. You can check this by looking at the lower right hand corner of QGIS Desktop and ensuring that EPSG: 2903 (OTF) is listed. If not right click on the parcels layer and from the context menu choose Set Project CRS from Layer.

8. Save the project to the Exercise 3 Data folder and name it exercise3.qgs.

9. From the menu bar choose Plugins | Manage and Install Plugins.

10. The Plugins manager will open. Options along the left side allow you to switch between Installed, Not Installed, New, and Settings. The plugin you will use is a Core QGIS Plugin called Georeferencer GDAL.

11. Since it is a Core plugin it will already be installed—you just need to enable it. Click on Installed plugins and check the box next to Georeferencer GDAL (shown in figure below).

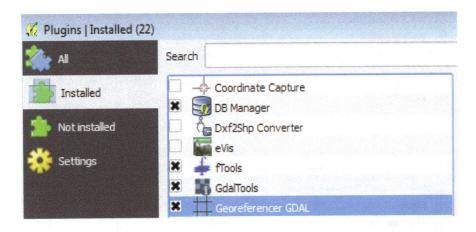

12. Click Close to close the Plugins window.

13. To open the Georeferencer plugin go to the menu bar choose Raster | Georeferencer | Georeferencer.

14. The Georeferencer window opens. Click the Open Raster button at the upper left hand side (see figure below).

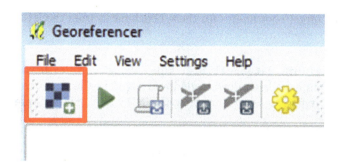

15. Navigate to the **Exercise 3 Data** folder and select the **zone_map.bmp** and click Open. *Note:* If the Coordinate Reference System Selector window opens click Cancel to close. This dataset does not yet have an Earth-based coordinate system. The source data will now be loaded in the Georeferencer (shown in figure below).

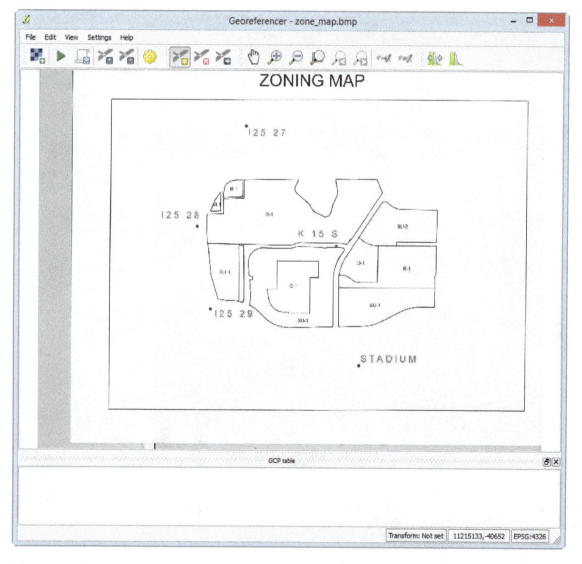

The source data is a map. On the map, there are five points with their associated names (for example, one point's name is: I25 27). These are benchmarks maintained by the National Geodetic Survey. To georeference this scanned map, you will create control points at these five locations. The plugin will then develop a georeferencing equation based off the set of source and target coordinates at these five locations. QGIS will obtain the source coordinates from your mouse click on those points. You will look up the target coordinates for these benchmarks from the NGS website.

16. The NGS website is at http://www.ngs.noaa.gov/cgi-bin/datasheet.prl. Open the site. *Note*: If you are unable to access the internet, the NGS Data Sheets have been downloaded and saved in the **Exercise 3 Data/NGS Data Sheets** folder. Please read the next few steps to learn how the NGS Data Sheets were acquired.

You will search for each of the benchmarks that appear on the map by searching for each benchmark's datasheet. You will use the Station Name option to do the search.

17. On the website click on the **DATASHEETS** button. Then click on the link for Station Name.

18. To find the first station, enter the station name of I25 27 (include the space), and then choose NEW MEXICO for the state. The search is shown in the figure below. *Note*: the station name is I25 27 with a capitalized letter i.

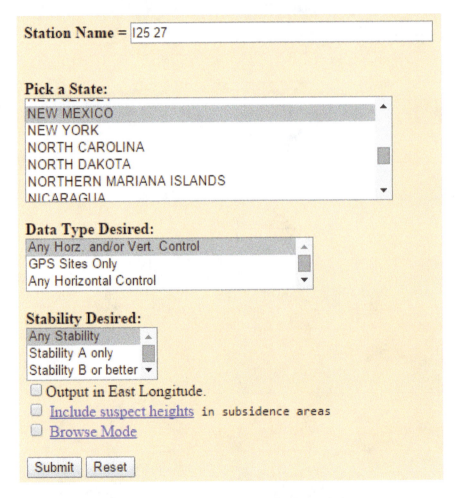

The search should return the page shown in the figure below.

Station List Results for: NM-I25 27

Help

```
|Dist|PID...|H V|Vert_Source|Latitude.....|Longitude.....|Stab|C|Designation ▲
|----|------|- -|-----------|-------------|--------------|----|-|-----------
|....|FO1302|2 3|29/LEVELING|N350445.73582|W1063813.49687|C...|G|I25  27
```

19. Highlight the station name and click the **Get Datasheets** button and you will get something that looks like the figure below.

The NGS Data Sheet

See file dsdata.txt for more information about the datasheet.

```
PROGRAM = datasheet95, VERSION = 8.6.1
1          National Geodetic Survey,   Retrieval Date = MARCH  9, 2015
 FO1302 *************************************************************************
 FO1302  DESIGNATION -  I25 27
 FO1302  PID         -  FO1302
 FO1302  STATE/COUNTY-  NM/BERNALILLO
 FO1302  COUNTRY     -  US
 FO1302  USGS QUAD   -  ALBUQUERQUE WEST (1990)
 FO1302
 FO1302                         *CURRENT SURVEY CONTROL
 FO1302  _____
 FO1302* NAD 83(1992) POSITION- 35 04 45.73582(N) 106 38 13.49687(W)   ADJUSTED
 FO1302* NAVD 88 ORTHO HEIGHT -  1545.38  (+/-2cm)      5070.1   (feet) VERTCON
 FO1302  _____
 FO1302  GEOID HEIGHT    -            -21.35  (meters)                GEOID12A
 FO1302  LAPLACE CORR    -              7.34  (seconds)               DEFLEC12A
 FO1302  HORZ ORDER      -  SECOND
 FO1302  VERT ORDER      -  THIRD ? (See Below)
 FO1302
 FO1302.The horizontal coordinates were established by classical geodetic methods
 FO1302.and adjusted by the National Geodetic Survey in December 1993.
 FO1302.
 FO1302.The NAVD 88 height was computed by applying the VERTCON shift value to
 FO1302.the NGVD 29 height (displayed under SUPERSEDED SURVEY CONTROL.)
 FO1302
 FO1302.The vertical order pertains to the NGVD 29 superseded value.
 FO1302
 FO1302.The Laplace correction was computed from DEFLEC12A derived deflections.
 FO1302
 FO1302. The following values were computed from the NAD 83(1992) position.
 FO1302
 FO1302;                    North        East     Units Scale Factor Converg.
 FO1302;SPC NM C    -     452,447.391  464,701.544   MT  0.99991535  -0 13 20.9
 FO1302;SPC NM C    -   1,484,404.48 1,524,608.32   sFT  0.99991535  -0 13 20.9
 FO1302;UTM  13     -   3,883,070.670  350,750.959   MT  0.99987453  -0 56 27.7
```

This is an NGS Data Sheet. It gives measurement parameters for NGS benchmarks located throughout the United States. One piece of information it includes are coordinates for benchmarks in State Plane feet (highlighted in the figure above). There are two sets of State Plane coordinates on the NGS Data Sheet; one is in meters (MT) and one is in feet (sFT). Be sure to use the set in feet. *Important Note*: There is a dash before the North coordinate. It is *not* a negative number.

20. Find the data sheet for each benchmark shown in the map and fill in the coordinates below. The coordinates for the first station have been entered already. *Note*: If you are unable to access the internet, the NGS Data Sheets have been downloaded and saved in the `Exercise 3 Data/NGS Data Sheets` folder.

```
Benchmark | Northing      | Easting
I25 27       1,484,404.48    1,524,608.32

I25 28

I25 29

K 15 S

STADIUM
```

21. The next step is to enter the control points in the Georeferencer. Click on the **Add point** button .

It is important to be precise and click directly on the point. To help make your selection more precise, you can zoom and pan by using tools in the View toolbar (shown in figure below). If you want to redo a control point click the **Delete point** button   then click on the point to delete.)

22. With the **Add point** button selected, click on point I25 27.

23. The **Enter map coordinates** window opens. Enter the easting and northing State Plane Coordinates that you retrieved from the NGS Data Sheet into the two boxes. Make sure you enter them correctly. The correct coordinates are entered for I25 27 in the figure below.

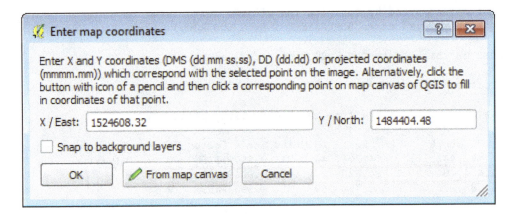

24. Click OK and a red control point will appear on the map where you clicked. The source (srcX, srcY) and

destination (dstX, dstY) X,Y coordinates will display in a table at the bottom of the window.

25. Repeat this procedure for points 'I25 28', I25 29', K 15 S' and 'STADIUM'. After the five control points have been entered your Georeferencer window should look like the figure below.

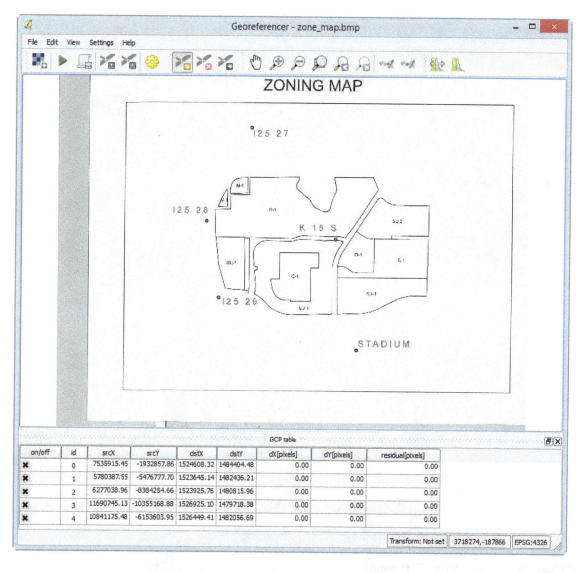

26. To perform the transformation click the **Start georeferencing** button ▶.

27. The **Transformation settings** window will open (see figure below). If beforehand you get a message saying 'Please set transformation' type click OK.

   a. In the Transformation window choose the Polynomial 1 as the Transformation type.

   b. Choose **Nearest neighbor** as the Resampling method. This is the standard raster resampling method for discrete data such as a scanned map.

   c. Click the browse button to the right of **Target SRS**. Type 2903 into the Filter.

   d. Click the NAD83(HARN)/New Mexico Central (ftUS):2903 CRS then click OK.

   e. Click the browse button to the right of **Output raster**. Navigate to your **Exercise 3 Data** folder.

   f. Create a new folder named **New Data** then enter the folder.

   g. Name the file **zone_map_modified_spcs.tif** and click Save.

   h. Check **Load in QGIS** when done.

i. Click OK to close the Transformation settings window and perform the transformation.

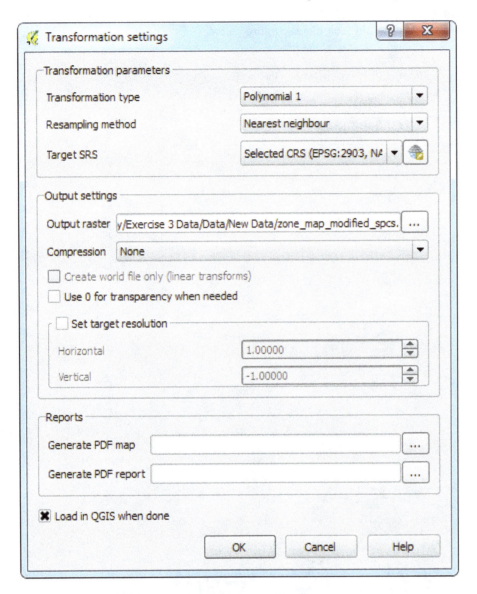

28. Close the Georeferencer and Save GCP points when prompted.

29. Right click on the `zone_map_modified.tif` and choose Zoom to layer extent to see the georeferenced image.

30. Using the **Add Vector Layer** button, add the `netcurr.shp` shapefile in the **Exercise 3 Data** folder to QGIS. This is a shapefile representing city streets produced by the City of Albuquerque. If the transformation was done correctly, the streets will line up with the georeferenced parcel map image (shown in figure below). Save your map file.

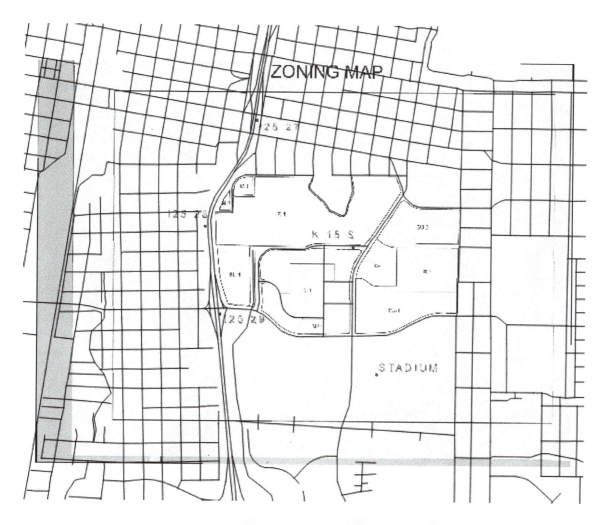

3.5   Task 3 - Heads-up Digitizing From Transformed Source Data

Now you will digitize the parcels off the georeferenced image into the parcels shapefile.

1. Drag the parcels layer above the zone_map_modified_spcs layer in the Layers panel. Right click on parcels and choose **Toggle editing**. This puts the parcels layer into edit mode. Notice that a pencil appears next to the layer in the Layers panel indicating that layer is in edit mode. Only one layer can be edited at a time.

2. Turn off the netcurr layer's visibility.

3. Using the **Zoom in** tool, drag a box around the M-1 parcels in the northwest corner of the image. You will digitize these first.

There is an Editing toolbar for editing vector datasets (see figure below). If it's not visible, go to the menu bar to View | **Toolbars** and turn it on. The tools available change slightly depending on the geometry of the data you are editing (polygon, line, point). When editing a polygon layer you will have a tool for adding polygon features.

4. Click on the **Add Feature** tool  . Your cursor will change to an editing cursor that looks like a set of cross hairs.

Polygons are constructed of a series of nodes which define their shape. Here you will trace the outline of the first parcel clicking to create each node on the polygons boundary.

5. Put your cursor over a corner of one of the polygons. Left click to add the first point, left click again to add the second, and continue to click around the perimeter of the parcel. After you have added the final node finish the polygon with a right click.

6. An Attributes window will open asking you to populate the two attributes for this layer: id and zonecode. Give the parcel an id of 0 and the zonecode is M-1 (shown in figure below). Each parcel feature will receive a unique id starting here with zero. The next parcel you digitize will be id 1, the one after that id 2 etc.

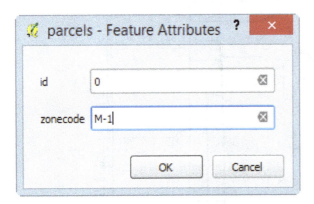

7. Click OK to close the Attributes window and complete the polygon.

If you want to delete the polygon you have just added, click the **Current Edits** tool dropdown menu and choose **Roll Back Edits** to undo your polygon.

8. Adding single isolated polygons is pretty straightforward. Zoom back to the extent of the image. You can do this by clicking the **Zoom last** button 🔍 .

9. Find the big parcel in the south central area. There is a parcel with zoning code SU-1 that wraps around O-1. Zoom to that area.

10. Open the **Layer properties | Style** tab for the parcels layer and set the **Transparency** to 50%. This will allow you to see the source data underneath your parcels as you digitize.

11. Digitize the outer boundary of the SU-1 parcel ignoring the O-1 parcel for the moment. Fill in the attributes when prompted (id=0, zonecode=SU-1). The SU-1 polygon will be a ring when completed but for now it covers the O-1 parcel.

12. To finish SU-1 you will use a tool on the Advanced Digitizing toolbar. To turn that on, go to the menu bar, choose **View | Toolbars**, and check Advanced Digitizing. Dock the Advanced Digitizing toolbar where you would like, as shown in figure below (all toolbars in the QGIS interface can be moved by grabbing the stippled left side and dragging them to different parts of the interface.)

13. Now you'll use the **Add Ring tool** 🔵 . Select it and click around the perimeter of the O-1 parcel. Right click to finish. This creates a ring polygon (shown in figure below).

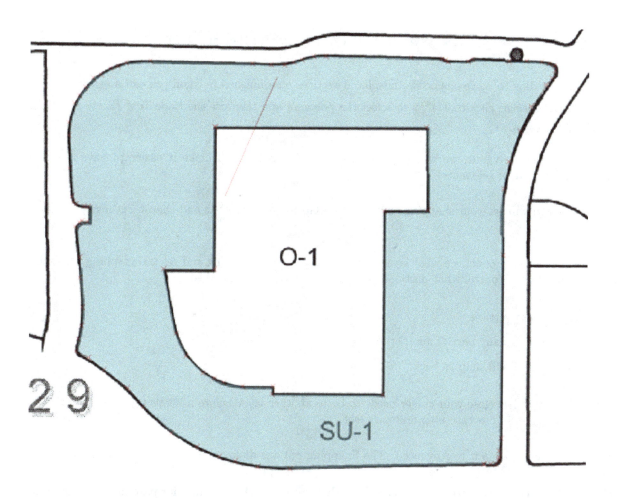

14. To Digitize O-1 you will use a tool that is part of the Digitizing Tools Plugin. First open the Plugin Manager and search for 'Digitizing Tools' in the All category. Select the Plugin and click the Install Plugin button. You should get the message *Plugin Installed Successfully*. Once it has been installed switch to the Installed plugins and make sure the Digitizing Tools toolbar is visible. Dock the toolbar.

15. On the Attributes toolbar, click the Select Features by area or single click tool and select the SU-1 polygon.

16. On the Digitizing toolbar, select the dropdown next to the Fill ring with a new feature (interactive mode) tool and select Fill all rings in selected polygons with new features tool (selection shown in figure below).

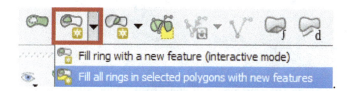

17. You will immediately be prompted to enter the attributes for the new O-1 polygon (id=2, zonecode=O-1).

18. Click OK when done and the new polygon will appear. It automatically fills the space leaving no gaps.

19. Use the Identify tool 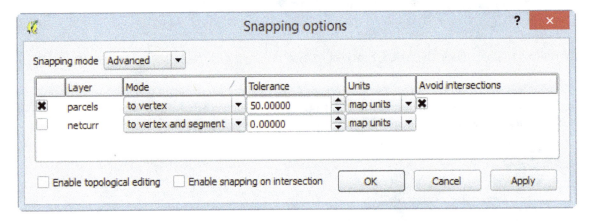 to click on O-1 and SU-1 and verify that they are digitized correctly.

Note: If you end up needing to move one or two misplaced vertices on a finished polygon you can do that. Use the Select Features by area or single click tool ⬚ to select the polygon, and then use the Node Tool ✎ to select the individual node and move it.

To digitize the remaining polygons, we will first turn on snapping options to make it easier to have adjacent polygons share vertices and/or segments.

20. To do so, first you will set your snapping environment. Go to the menu bar and choose Settings | Snapping options.

This is a window that lets you configure what layers you can snap to while editing and set the snapping tolerance. The Snapping mode lets you control what portions of a feature are being snapped to.

- To vertex will snap to vertices

- To segment will snap to any part of another layers edge

- To vertex and segment will snap to both.

The Tolerance determines how close your cursor needs to be to another layer before it snaps to it. It can be set in screen pixels or map units. In our case map units are feet.

21. For Snapping mode, change it to Advanced. The Snapping options dialog will now show a list of map layers and options.

22. Check `parcels` since we want to snap our parcels to that layer. Set the tolerance for parcels to 50 map units and choose a Mode of 'to vertex'.

23. Check the box under Avoid intersections to the right of Units (shown in the figure below). This enables topological editing. When digitizing a shared boundary with this option checked you can begin with one of the vertices at one end of the shared boundary. Then continue digitizing the boundary of the new polygon and end at a vertex at the other end of the shared boundary. The shared boundary will be created automatically eliminating digitizing errors.

	Layer	Mode /	Tolerance	Units	Avoid intersections
☒	parcels	to vertex ▼	50.00000 ▲▼	map units ▼	☒
☐	netcurr	to vertex and segment ▼	0.00000 ▲▼	map units ▼	

Snapping mode Advanced ▼

☐ Enable topological editing   ☐ Enable snapping on intersection   [OK]   [Cancel]   [Apply]

Snapping options

The map units are feet so when you get within 50 feet of a node (vertex) you will snap to it. This allows you to be much more precise than you could be otherwise.

24. Click OK to set the Snapping options.

If snapping is interfering with digitizing a parcel polygon you can go to Settings | Snapping options at any time (even during digitizing) and turn snapping off until you need it again.

25. Finish digitizing the polygons. Anytime you have a parcel that shares a boundary with another, use snapping to make sure you create two parcels without a gap in between.

Remember, you can adjust the snapping tolerance and what features are being snapped to vertex, segment, and vertex and segment.

26. When finished, click the Toggle Editing 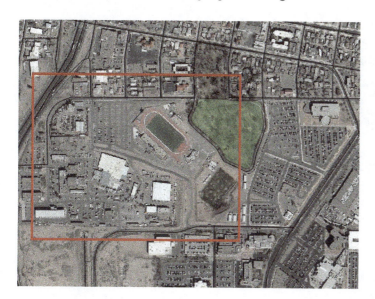 button to exit out of editing mode. You will be prompted to save your changes. Click Save to save the edits.

27. Turn off the zone_map_modified_spcs raster—you're done with that now. It was an intermediate step necessary to get the parcel boundaries digitized.

28. Save your QGIS project.

3.6 Task 4 - Editing Existing Geospatial Data

Now that you have digitized data into the empty shapefile you created, you will learn how to modify existing shapefiles.

1. Click the Add Raster Layer button and navigate to the **Exercise 3 Data** folder.
2. Set the filter to Multi-resolution Seamless Image Database (.sid, .SID).
3. Add all four SID images.
4. Drag the parcels layer above the image in the Layers panel.
5. Turn off the parcels layer.
6. Now you will make an edit to a line layer. Turn on the netcurr layer.
7. Zoom into the location highlighted in Figure below.

You will digitize the missing main road, shown in yellow in the figure below.

8. Toggle on editing for netcurr.

9. Set your Snapping options so that only netcurr is being snapped to, with a Mode of To vertex and a Tolerance of 20 feet.

10. Using the Add Feature tool on the Editing toolbar [icon] , digitize the new road making sure to snap to the roads at the northern and southern ends. Use the centerline of the road while digitizing.

11. There are many attributes for this layer. You will just enter a few. Enter the STREETNAME as Park, the STREETDESI as Place, the STREETQUAD as SE and the COMMENTS as Exercise 5. Click OK.

12. Toggle off editing and Save.

3.7 Conclusion

In this exercise, you have successfully digitized information using the five-step digitizing process. Additionally, you have recreated the original source data (scanned as a raster) in the vector format. Digitizing can be a time-consuming and tedious process, but can yield useful geographic information.

3.8 Discussion Questions

1. What can contribute to errors in the georeferencing process?

2. What other vector geometries (point/line/polygon) could be appropriate for digitizing a road? In which instances would you use one vector geometry type over another?

3. When you created the parcels shapefile you added a text field to hold the zoning codes. What are the possible field types? Explain what each field type contains, and provide an example of a valid entry in the field.

4. Aerial photography has a lot of information in it. What other features could you digitize from the imagery in this exercise? Explain what vector geometry you would use for each.

3.9 Challenge Assignment (optional)

You have successfully created the parcel data from a scanned map. You have also fixed the roads data in this part of town. There are some sports facilities visible: two football fields and a baseball field. Create a new layer and digitize those three facilities (include the grassy field areas at a minimum).

Create a simple page sized color map composition using the QGIS Desktop Print Composer showing your results. Show the parcels, sports facilities, parks, roads and aerial photography. Use Categorized styling to give a unique color to each zone code in the parcel data. Include:

- Title

- Legend (be sure to rename your layers so that the legend will be meaningful.)

- Date and Data Sources

You can credit the data sources as the City of Albuquerque and yourself. If you need to refresh your memory on creating a map layout, review Exercise 2.

Exercise 4

Understanding Remote Sensing and Analysis

Objective – Explore and Understand How to Display and Analyze Remotely Sensed Imagery

4.1 Introduction

In this exercise, you'll learn how to display and inspect multiband imagery in QGIS Desktop, then use QGIS data processing tools to conduct an unsupervised classification of multispectral imagery.

This exercise includes the following tasks:

- Task 1 – Display and Inspection of Image Data

- Task 2 – Unsupervised Classification

4.2 Objective: Learn the Basics of using QGIS Desktop for Image Analysis

Image analysis is one of the largest uses of remote sensing imagery, especially with imagery that has recorded wavelengths beyond the visible spectrum. There are proprietary software packages designed specifically for remote sensing work such as ENVI and ERDAS Imagine. QGIS Desktop can now be used in combination with two additional FOSS4G applications, SAGA and GRASS, to also conduct image analysis. SAGA and GRASS are both standalone software packages that can be installed separately. However, the main analysis tools from both are now bundled with QGIS Desktop. This means that no additional installations are required in order to use GRASS and SAGA analysis tools via QGIS Desktop. Some of this functionality is for more advanced users.

4.3 Task 1 - Display and Inspection of Image Data

There are many way to view multiband image data. Here you will explore some display options for a multiband image in QGIS Desktop.

1. Open QGIS Desktop and open the `Exercise_4_MultiSpectral_Imagery.qgs` project file.

2. The project contains is an aerial photograph of a portion of the Davis Purdue Agriculture Center in Randolph County, Indiana.

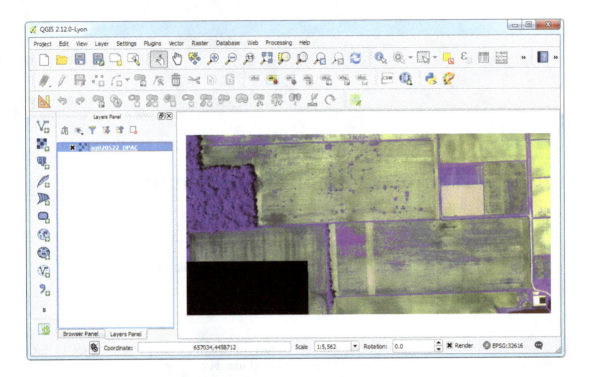

3. Double click on the layer name in the Layers panel to open the **Layer Properties**. Click on the **General** tab.

Layer info shows you the layer name, where the data are stored on your computer, and the number of columns (1,501) and rows (709). Since the CRS for the image is set when you added it to QGIS, the CRS is listed under Coordinate Reference System. Scale dependent visibility allows you to control at what scales the layer is visible. You will not set this parameter here. If you wanted the image to be visible only at a certain scale range, you could check the box and enter a scale maximum and minimum.

4. Click on the **Style** tab.

This image has three bands. Each band represents a segment of the electromagnetic spectrum. In this case, band 1 represents the red portion, band 2 the green portion, and band 3 the near-infrared portion. Therefore, in this image, we are able to see characteristics of the landscape that we cannot see with our eyes, since they can only detect visible light.

When an image has multiple color bands, QGIS defaults to a Multiband color rendering of that image. Colors on your computer monitor are created by combining three color channels: red, green and blue (RGB). By selecting three bands from a multiband image, and illuminating them with either red, green or blue light we create a color image. The multiband color renderer defaults to displaying Band 1 through the red channel, Band 2 through the green channel and Band 3 through the blue channel. However, we can change which bands are displayed through which channels.

5. Click the drop-down arrow for the Red band and change it to Band 3. Change the Blue band to Band 1 (see figure below).

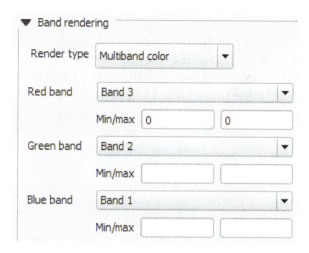

6. Click Apply and move the Layer Properties window so you can see the raster.

Note: Here is the difference between using Apply and OK: clicking OK saves the changes and closes the dialog window while apply saves the changes and leaves the window open. If you want to change a setting, see the result and change another setting, use Apply.

7. The image should now look like the figure below. This band combination creates what is known as a false color composite. Vegetation reflects a lot of near-infrared energy. You are now looking at the near-infrared through the red channel so vegetation shows up as red tones. The brighter the red, the more vigorous and healthy the vegetation.

The **Style** tab also allows you to adjust **Contrast enhancement**. This setting gives you options to modify the appearance of the image when used in combination with the Load min/max values settings. Each band has values from 0-255. By default, the renderer is set to use **Cumulative count cut** values from 2% to 98%. This setting eliminates the bottom and top 2% of the values. Many images have some outlying very low and high data values. These outlying data values can be eliminated by using the **Cumulative count cut** option. The **Contrast enhancement** is set by default to **No enhancement**.

8. Click the **Load** button. The values currently being used for each band will appear in the Min/max boxes in

the Band rendering area.

9. Change the Contrast enhancement to Stretch to MinMax and click Apply. This setting scales the colors between the minimum and maximum values. The image gets a little brighter (see figure below) because the colors are now being stretched across the range of values. You are both applying a stretch and eliminating the bottom and top 2% of the values with the default Cumulative count cut setting.

The Accuracy setting lets you either estimate the range of values from a sample or get the actual values. Obtaining actual values can take longer since QGIS has to look at all the values in the image, instead of a sample.

10. Change the Accuracy setting to Actual, and click the Load button to see the values change slightly.

11. Now choose a Load min/max values setting of Mean +/- standard deviation and click Load. Click Apply to see the image change.

The raster gets a more saturated appearance (shown in figure below). These are the values within one standard deviation of the mean value. This is useful when you have one or two cells with abnormally high values in a raster grid that are having a negative impact on the rendering of the raster.

12. You can also look at one individual band. Change the Render type to Singleband gray. Choose Band 3 as the Gray band. Set the Contrast enhancement to Stretch MinMax. Click Apply.

13. Change the Gray band setting to each of the other two bands and see how different they look.

14. Change back to a false color composite view:

    a. Render type: Multiband color

    b. Red band = 3

    c. Green band = 2

    d. Blue band = 1

    e. Contrast enhancement = Stretch to MinMax

    f. Click Load

    g. Click Apply

    h. In the Layer Properties, click on the Transparency tab.

    i. With the Global transparency setting you can control the transparency of the entire image.

    j. You can also define image values that you want to be transparent. Notice that in the southwest corner there is a black rectangle with no image data. On the Transparency tab click the Add values from display button [icon] then click on the black rectangle on the map. QGIS will measure the values for all three bands where you clicked and enter them into the Transparent pixel list.

    k. Click Apply. The black rectangle of no data pixels disappears.

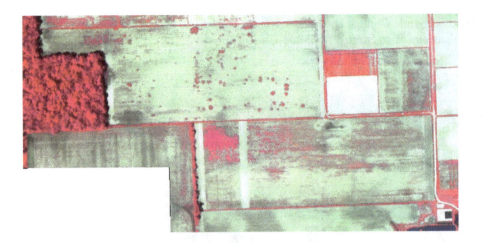

15. Click on the Pyramids tab.

Raster data sets can get very large. Pyramids help render large images more quickly. Without them, QGIS will try to render each pixel in an image even though your monitor may not have enough resolution to display each pixel. Pyramids are lower resolution versions of the image that will increase performance. This particular image is small so you will not build any now.

16. Click on the Histogram tab.

Here you can view the distribution of data values in your raster. If it is a multiband image, you can view data for each band. The histogram is generated automatically when you open this tab (see figure below). You can save the histogram as an image with the Save plot button.

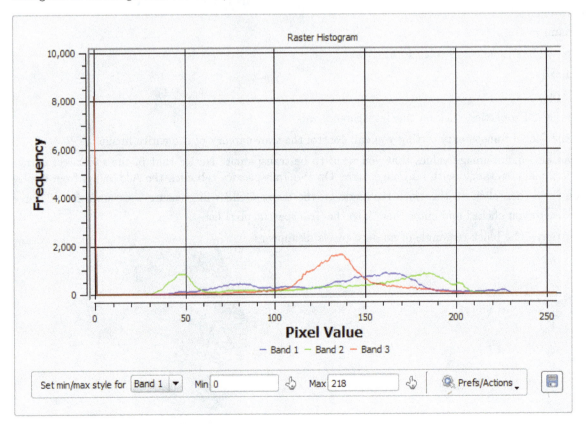

17. Save your QGIS Desktop project.

4.4   Task 2 - Unsupervised Classification

In an unsupervised classification, the software automatically classifies the image into homogenous areas. Pixels are grouped based on the reflectance values.

1. Open QGIS Desktop and then open the `Exercise 4 Data/ Exercise_4_Landsat.qgs` document.

2. This project contains a subset of a Landsat 8 scene covering Rome. There are separate rasters for bands 2, 3, 4, 5, 6, and 7. The image was acquired on June 12, 2014.

3. You will be using a Processing tool to conduct the unsupervised classification. From the menu bar, choose Processing | Toolbox to open the Processing Toolbox panel.

NOTE: Prior to QGIS version 2.14, the toolbox could be toggled between Simplifed and Advanced interfaces. At QGIS 2.14 the Simplified interface was removed. If using QGIS 2.12 or earlier, choose the Advanced interface.

1. Use the Search box at the top of the panel to help locate the tool. Type *cluster* into the Search box.

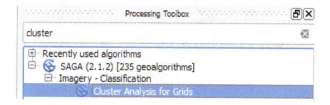

5. Double click on the SAGA tool Cluster Analysis for Grids.

6. Fill out the tool as follows (reference figure below):

   a. Click the ellipsis button to the right of Grids to open the Multiple Selection box. Click Select all and OK.

   b. Choose a Method of 2 Combined Minimum Distance/Hillclimbing

   c. Change the number of Clusters to 7.

   d. Click Run to run the cluster analysis. The result will be a temporary file.

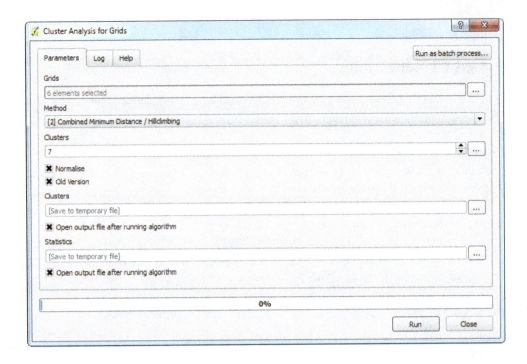

7. The temporary grid and a Statistics table are added to the Layers Panel. The Clusters grid will appear in the Map Window styled on a black to white color ramp.

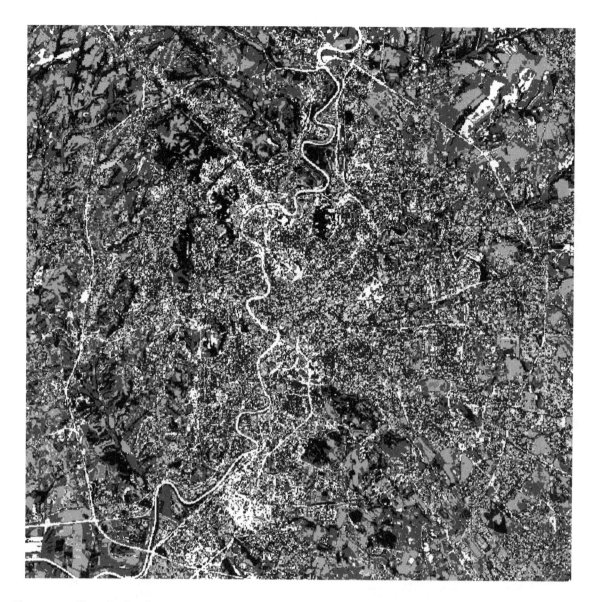

Now you will style the data.

8. Open Layer Properties for the new layer.

9. Change from a Singleband gray renderer to a Singleband pseudocolor render.

10. Change the Mode to Equal Interval.

11. Set the number of Classes to 6.

12. Change the Accuracy setting to Actual (slower) and click Load.

13. Click the Classify button.

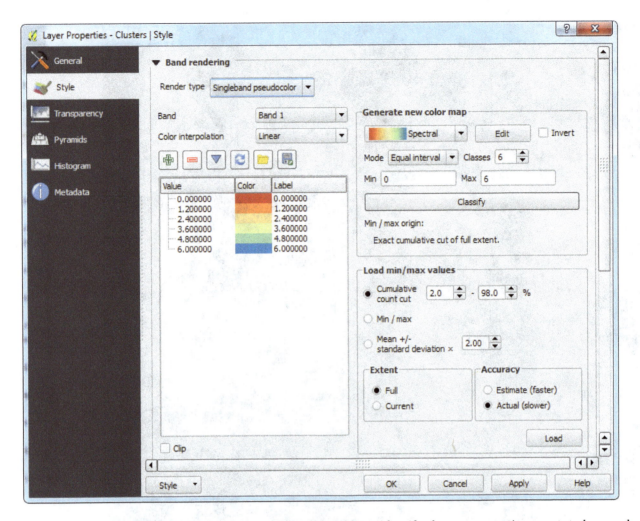

The data now shows the six classes of data. You will be able to identify those representing vegetated areas, barren soil, built up areas and water.

4.5   Conclusion

In this exercise, you have learned the basics of working with multispectral imagery in QGIS Desktop. You learned how to access data processing tools in QGIS Desktop and how to do an Unsupervised Classification.

4.6   Challenge Assignment (optional)

You have used QGIS to perform an Unsupervised Classification of the multispectral imagery. Create a simple page sized color map composition using the QGIS Desktop Print Composer showing your results. Include:

- Title

- Legend (be sure to rename your layers so that the legend will be meaningful.)

- Date and Data Sources

You can credit the data sources as the U.S. Geologic Survey and yourself. If you need to refresh your memory, review Exercise 2.

Exercise 5

Basic Geospatial Analysis Techniques

Objective – Use Basic Spatial Analysis Techniques to Solve a Problem

5.1 Introduction

In this exercise, the you'll explore a small set of analysis tools available in QGIS Desktop to conduct a spatial analysis and create a map of the results for a team of surveyors visiting National Geodetic Survey Monuments in Albuquerque, New Mexico. The surveyors wish to have a map showing monuments within the Albuquerque city limits. They will use this map to plan their fieldwork for the week.

This exercise includes the following tasks:

- Task 1 – Data Preparation
- Task 2 – Querying and Extracting Subsets of Data
- Task 3 – Buffering and Clipping Data
- Task 4 – Preparing a Map

5.2 Objective: Use Basic Spatial Analysis Techniques to Solve a Problem

Conducting effective spatial analysis in a GIS does not require the use of extremely complex algorithms and methods. By combining multiple simple spatial analysis operations, you can answer many questions and provide useful results. Determining the order in which these simple spatial analysis operations are executed is often the hardest part of conducting spatial analysis. Additionally, data is rarely available in exactly the format and subset that you require. A large part of almost all GIS projects is simply obtaining and preparing data for use.

In this exercise, the you'll utilize four basic geospatial analysis techniques: selection, buffer, clip, and dissolve.

- Selection uses set algebra and Boolean algebra to select records of interest.
- Buffer is the definition of a region that is less than or equal to a distance from one or more features.
- Clip defines the areas for which features will be output based on a 'clipping' polygon.
- Dissolve combines similar features within a data layer based on an attribute.

5.3   Task 1 - Data Preparation

In this task, you will obtain GIS data for this exercise by visiting several online GIS data portals, A) the National Geodetic Survey (NGS) website, B) City of Albuquerque GIS Department, C) the New Mexico Resource Geographic Information System (RGIS) and D) the Bernalillo County GIS Department. All of these websites provide free geospatial information.

Note: Copies of this data have already been obtained and are available in the Exercise 5/Data/Raw Data folder. If you are unable to obtain the data yourself, you may skip to Task 2 and use the Raw Data.

5.4   Task 1.1 - Obtain Shapefiles of NGS Monuments

We first want to go to the same National Geodetic Survey (NGS) website you visited in exercise 5. This time you will download a shapefile of the monuments in the Bernalillo County, New Mexico. This is the county in which Albuquerque is situated.

1. In a web browser, navigate to http://www.ngs.noaa.gov
2. Click on the Survey Mark Datasheets link of the left side of the page.
3. Click the Shapefiles button.
4. Use the COUNTY retrieval method:

    a. Pick a State = New Mexico then click Get County List
    b. Pick a County = Bernalillo
    c. Data Type Desired = Any Vertical Control
    d. Stability Desired = Any Stability
    e. Compression Options = Send me all the Shapefiles compressed into one ZIP file...
    f. File Prefix = Bern
    g. (Leave all other options as the default values)
    h. Click the Submit button
    i. Click the Select All button
    j. Click Get Shapefile
    k. When the dialog box appears to save the ZIP file, save it into the `Exercise 5 Data/MyData` directory.
    l. Extract the ZIP file into the `MyData` directory.

5.5   Task 1.2 - Obtain the Municipal Boundaries

Since you will identify monuments within the Albuquerque City limits, you'll need an Albuquerque City limit dataset. You will download the data from the City of Albuquerque GIS Department.

1. In a web browser, navigate to http://www.cabq.gov/gis/geographic-information-systems-data
2. Scroll down until you find the Municipal Limits data.
3. Download the Boundaries shapefile to your folder.

    a. Save the ZIP file into your `Exercise 5 Data/MyData` directory.
    b. Extract this ZIP file into the exercise directory.

5.6   Task 1.3 - Obtain the Census Tract Boundaries

You will visit the RGIS clearinghouse. This is the main source for geospatial data for New Mexico. You will download census tract boundaries for Bernalillo County.

1. In a web browser, navigate to http://rgis.unm.edu/
2. Click the Get Data button
3. In the folder tree underneath Filter data by Theme, expand Census Data
4. Expand 2010 Census
5. Click on 2010 Census Tracts
6. Download the Bernalillo County 2010 Census Tracts shapefile to your folder.
   a. Save the ZIP file into your `Exercise 5 Data/MyData` directory.
   b. Extract this ZIP file into the exercise directory.

5.7   Task 1.4 - Obtain Road Data

Finally, you will visit the Bernalillo County GIS Program to download a roads data set. This is the main source for geospatial data for New Mexico. You will download census tract boundaries for Bernalillo County.

1. In a web browser, navigate to http://www.bernco.gov/Download-GIS-Data/
2. Find the Download GIS data section
3. Find Road Inventory
4. Download the Road Inventory Zip file to your folder.
   a. Save the ZIP file into your `Exercise 5/MyData` directory.
   b. Extract this ZIP file into the exercise directory.

5.8   Task 2 - Querying and Extracting Subsets of Data

Now that you have collected the necessary data, you will add it to a blank QGIS map document. Take a moment to familiarize yourself with the data and what information it contains. As with any project, you will have to do some data preparation to make it useful for the analysis.

5.9   Task 2.1 - Working with coordinate reference systems

1. Open QGIS Desktop.
2. Using the Add Vector Layer button, add all four shapefiles to QGIS Desktop (see figure below).

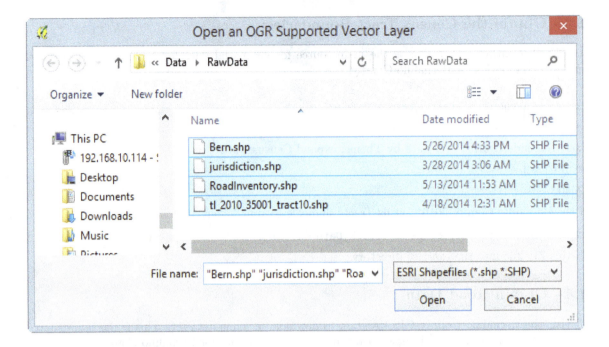

3. Organize the layers in the Layers panel so that the Bern monuments layer is on top, followed by the Road-Inventory, tl_2010_35001_tract10 (tracts), and jurisdiction.

4. Save your project to the **Exercise 5 Data** folder as `exercise5.qgs`

Does it look like all the layers are lining up together? Open the Layer properties for each layer and investigate their CRSs. Note that the Census Tracts (tl_2010_35001_tract10) and Monuments (Bern) are in geographic coordinates and the Road Inventory and jurisdiction are in the State Plane Coordinate System (SPCS).

5. From the menu bar choose **Project | Project Properties**.

6. Open the CRS tab and note that 'on the fly' CRS Transformation is checked. This is the default behavior if QGIS notices that Layers in the Layers panel have different CRSs. To change this default behavior, from the main menu bar, click **Settings | Options | CRS** tab and choose the default CRS settings.

7. While the CRS tab is still open choose NAD83(HARN)/New Mexico Central (ftUS) as the CRS for the map (EPSG: 2903).

8. Click OK to set the project CRS.

Projecting on the fly is fine for cartographic purposes. However, when conducting a geospatial analysis, the data layers involved should be in the same CRS. Typically, data layers will also be clipped to the extent of the study area to reduce rendering and data processing time. These procedures are often referred to as normalizing your data. For the typical analysis, a majority of your time is spent obtaining data and normalizing it. Once all the data is organized and normalized, the analysis can proceed.

You will want to put all four layers into the same CRS for this analysis. You will put them all into the SPCS.

9. Right-click on the Bern layer in the Layers panel and choose **Save As...** from the contextual menu. This will open the **Save vector layer as...** window (shown in the figure below).

10. Click the **Browse** button to the right of **Save as** and save it into your exercise folder as `Bern_spcs.shp`. (It is useful to have a naming convention for new data layers. Here you are including the CRS in the name of the copy.)

11. Click the **Browse** button for the CRS. The Coordinate Reference System Selector window will open.

12. From the Recently used coordinate reference systems choose NAD83(HARN) / New Mexico Central (ftUS) EPSG:2903 then click OK.

13. Check the box for Add saved file to map.

14. Click OK to save the new file in a different CRS.

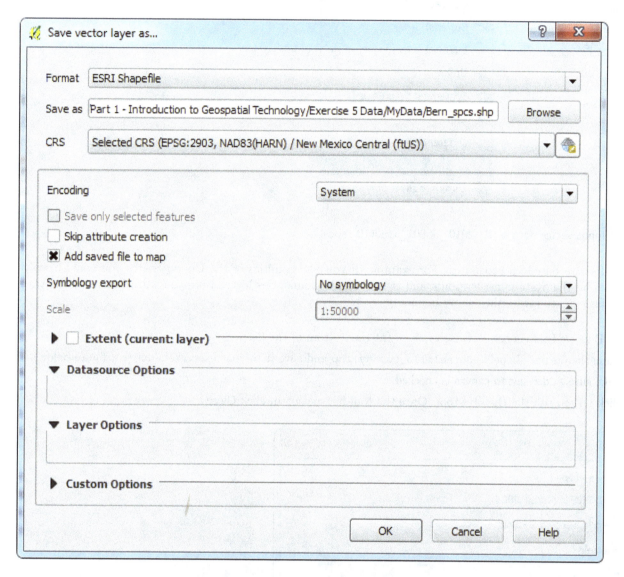

15. You no longer need the original Bern layer in your map. Right-click on the original Bern layer and choose Remove. Click OK on the Remove Objects window.

16. Repeat the above steps to save the Census Tracts (tl_2010_35001_tract10) layer in EPSG:2903.

17. Save your project.

5.10   Task 2.2 - Dissolving Tract Boundaries into a County boundary

For the map, you will need a polygon that represents the county boundary. The tl_2010_35001_tract10_spcs Census tracts collectively define the county, so you will use the dissolve spatial analysis technique to create a county boundary from the Census tracts.

1. From the menu bar choose Vector | Geoprocessing Tools | Dissolve (reference figure below).

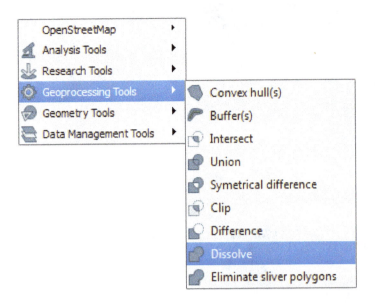

2. Set Input vector data to tl_2010_35001_tract10_spcs.

You can dissolve based on attributes. For example, if you had counties of the United States you could dissolve them based on the State name attribute and create a state boundaries layer. Here you will dissolve all the tract polygons into one to create the county boundary.

3. For Dissolve field choose — Dissolve all — (at the bottom of the list).

4. Name the output shapefile `Bernalillo_county.shp` and save it to your exercise folder (see figure below).

5. Make sure Add result to canvas is checked.

6. Click OK to run the Dissolve tool. Once the tool has executed, click Close.

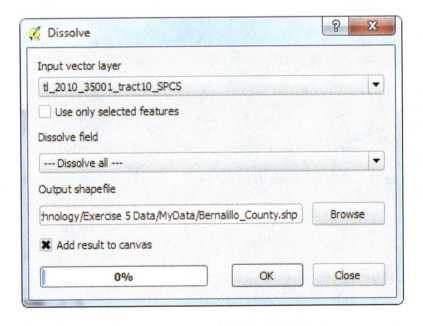

7. Remove the tl_2010_35001_tract10_spcs layer from the Layers panel. It was an intermediate dataset. All you need is the Bernalillo County Boundary.

8. Save your project.

5.11   Task 2.3 - Select Monuments

You will want to filter the monuments so that you only have the ones with the orders and classes you're interested in. Here you only want monuments that meet the following requirements:

- Elevation Order = 1

- Last recovered on or after 1995

- Satellite Observations were used for monument coordinate determination.

- a, b, and c are stored in these attribute columns:
    - ELEV_ORDER
    - LAST_RECV
    - SAT_USE

(For information on what an elevation order and class is, visit http://www.ngs.noaa.gov/heightmod/Leveling/)

1. Double-click the Bern_spcs layer to open the Layer Properties.
2. Select the General tab.
3. Find the Provider feature filter subset area. This is where you can define the contents of a layer based on the attributes. It is a way to filter a layer.
4. Click the Query Builder button to open the Query Builder. Here you can write a SQL query to filter your data.

All the attribute fields are listed on the left. Below the fields are operators you can use to build your SQL expression. The expression is built in the blank window at the bottom. When building the expression, it is best to double-click fields and field values instead of manually typing them in so that you avoid syntax errors.

5. Double-click on the field ELEV_ORDER and it will appear in the expression window surrounded by double quotes.
6. Click the = sign under operators to add it to the expression.
7. Click the All button below Values to get a list of the values contained in that field.
8. Double-click the 1 value so that your expression reads "ELEV_ORDER" = '1'.

Since you want monuments that have both an elevation order of 1 and were last recovered on or after 1994 you will now use the AND operator. The AND operator selects records that meet conditions on both sides.

9. Double-click the AND button under Operators to add it to the expression.
10. After the AND operator create the portion of the expression dealing with LAST_RECV.
11. Add another AND operator and create the third portion of the expression dealing with the SAT_USE.
12. The final expression should look like the figure below.

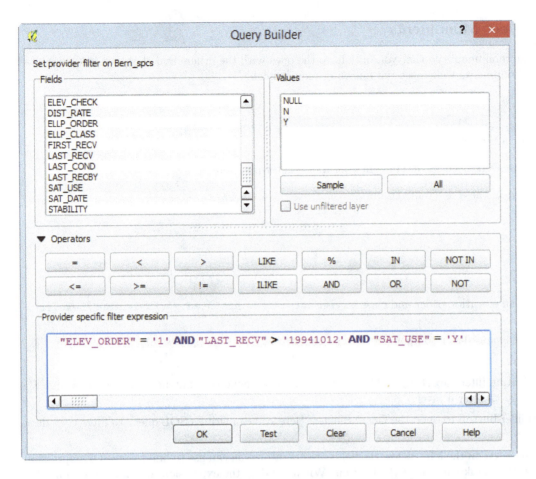

13. Click the **Test** button. You should get a query result of 47 rows. If you have a syntax error you will be notified and you'll have to figure out where the error lies. Any extra tics (') or quotes (") will throw an error. Click OK to dismiss the query result dialog.

14. Click OK to set the Query and close the Query Builder window.

15. Click OK again to close the Layer Properties.

It is always a good idea to open the attribute table to ensure that the layer has been filtered the way you needed.

16. Open the attribute table for the Bern_spcs layer and verify that the table only includes 47 filtered features. This will be reported on the attribute table's title bar at the top.

17. With the data properly filtered, the map should now resemble the figure below.

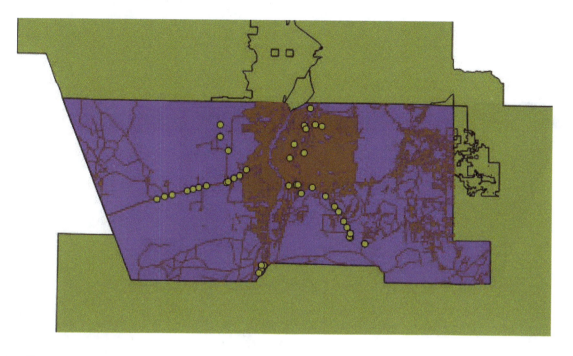

18. Save your project.

5.12   Task 3 - Buffering and Clipping Data

Now that you have prepared the county boundary and the monuments layers, you will identify just the monuments within the Albuquerque City limits. First, you will create a filter on the jurisdiction layer and the RoadInventory layer as you did for monuments.

The jurisdiction layer covers much more than Bernalillo County. Albuquerque covers just a portion of the county and jurisdiction extends north and south of the county boundary.

1. Open the attribute table for jurisdiction. The first field JURISDICTI has the city names. Notice that the majority consists of unincorporated areas. You can click the field header and you will see a small arrow appear. This lets you toggle back and forth between an ascending and descending sort of the records making it easier to find certain values. Close the Table.

2. Open the Layer properties for jurisdiction and go to the General tab.

3. Under Provider feature filter subset, click the Query Builder button and create a query that selects only the JURISDICTI of Albuquerque.

4. Click OK on the Query Builder and close the Layer Properties.

5. In the Layers panel, drag jurisdiction above the Bernalillo County layer and turn off RoadInventory. Your map should resemble the figure below.

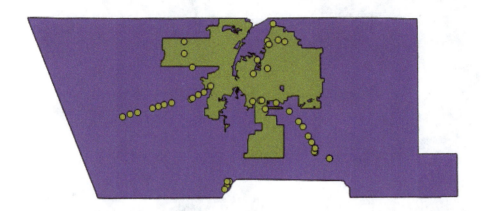

6. Open the attribute table for RoadInventory.

There is a lot of information in the RoadInventory shapefile. So far you have filtered a layer within QGIS, but left the data on disk the same. Now you will select the major roads and save them to a new shapefile. Considering the attribute table, what field would you use to select out major roads?

7. Click on the Select features using an expression button.

A similar query window opens as when you are filtering a layer. Instead of the fields being listed on the left, here you have the Expression area. In the middle, the expression functions will be listed. If you scroll down though the functions tree, you will see that one category is Fields and Values.

8. Expand Fields and Values.

9. Scroll down until you find the Class field.

10. Double-click on Class to add it to the Expression area.

11. Click the = operator.

12. Click all unique under Values.

13. Double-click the Major value to add it to the expression. Your expression should now look like the figure below.

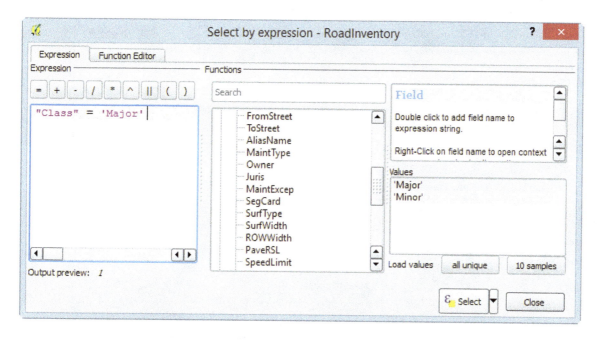

14. Click **Select** then **Close** the **Select by expression** window.

You now have 4,593 out of 37,963 records selected. You can use the dropdown at the lower left corner of the attribute table to show just the selected set of records (see figure below).

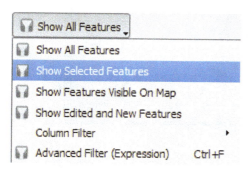

15. Close the attribute table.

16. Right-click on the RoadInventory layer and choose **Save As....**

17. Name the file `Major_Roads.shp` and save it in your exercise directory.

18. Check **Save only selected features.** The will only save the features currently selected to a new shapefile.

19. Verify that the dialog looks like the figure below. If so, click OK to save and add the layer to the map.

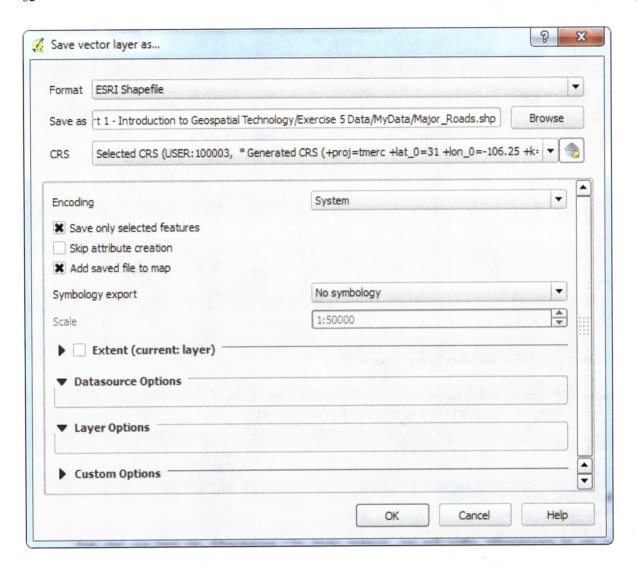

20. Remove RoadInventory from the Layers panel. All you need for your map is Major_Roads.

Now that you have the Albuquerque City limits isolated, you will buffer Albuquerque by one mile. This will allow you to identify monuments that are either inside, or close to the city limits. Buffer is an operation that creates a new polygon layer that is a buffer distance from another layer.

21. From the menu bar choose Vector | Geoprocessing Tools | Buffer(s).

22. Set the Input vector layer to jurisdiction, which now equals the Albuquerque city boundary.

23. You will enter a Buffer distance in map units. The Project CRS is a State Plane Coordinate System (SPCS), which has feet for units. Therefore, to buffer the city boundary by a mile, enter the number of feet in a mile (5280).

24. Name the output Albuquerque_buffer.shp.

25. Check Add result to canvas.

26. Your tool should resemble the figure below. If so, click OK and then Close.

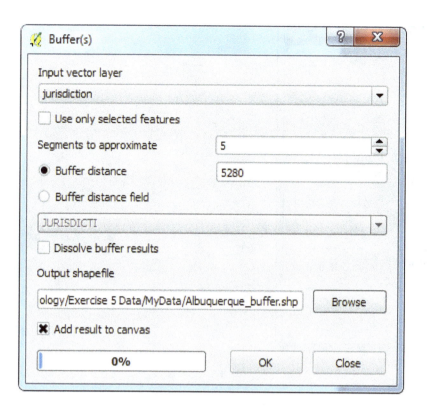

27. Drag the new buffer layer beneath jurisdiction and you will see that it is a one-mile buffer of the boundary.

Now that you have the search area for the selected monuments, you will use the Clip tool to clip the monument layer to the buffered city limits to create a new shapefile with only the monuments the surveyors should visit. The Clip tool acts like a cookie cutter. It cuts data out that falls within the clipping layer's boundary.

28. From the menu bar choose Vector | Geoprocessing Tools | Clip.

29. Set Input vector layer to Bern_spcs.

30. Set Clip layer to Albuquerque_buffer.

31. Name the output Albuquerque_monuments.shp.

32. Check Add result to canvas.

33. Your tool should resemble the figure below. If so, click OK and Close.

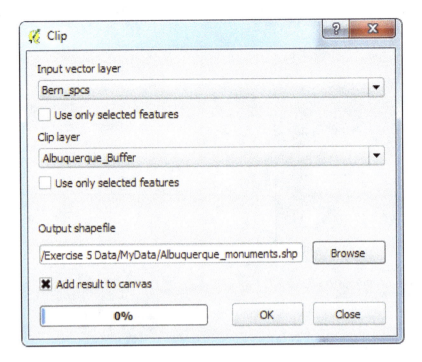

34. Remove Bern_spcs from the Layers panel.

Finally, you will label the monuments with the FeatureID attribute.

35. Open the Layer properties for the Albuquerque Monuments and select the **Labels** tab.

36. Check **Label with** and choose **FeatureId** as the field.

37. Select the **Buffer** item and check **Draw text buffer** with the defaults (reference figure below). This will create a white halo around the labels, which can make them easier to read against a busy background.

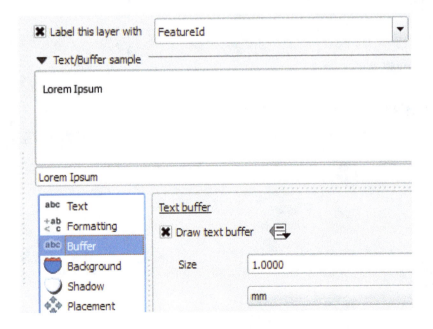

38. Click the **Placement** option and set an **Offset X,Y** of 2. This will offset the label from the point a bit giving more room for a bigger point symbol. Note that there are many options for label placement!

39. Click OK to set the labels for the monuments.

40. Label the major roads using the `StreetName` field. Under the `Text` tab, set a font size of 5.25.

41. On the Rendering tab, under the `Feature options` area, choose `Merge connected lines to avoid duplicate labels`. This will clean up duplicate labels.

42. Change the style of the layer to make the map more attractive. Choose whatever colors you prefer. As an example, reference the map in the figure below.

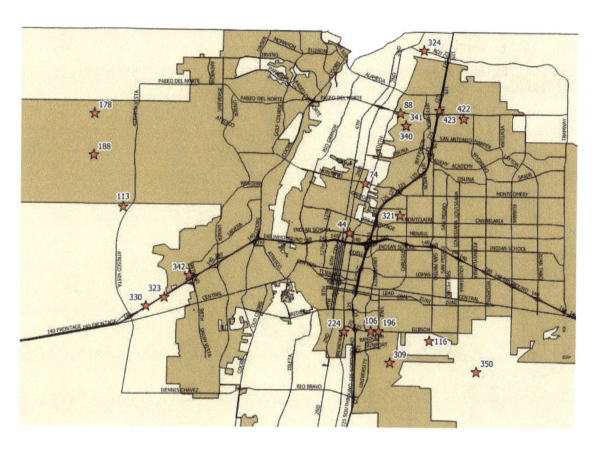

43. Save your project.

5.13   Task 4 - Preparing a Map

Now that you have identified the locations of the monuments that the surveyors should visit, you will make a map of the result of your analysis. You should show the major roads to give them a general idea of how to access the monuments.

1. Rename the layers in the Layers panel to:

   a. Albuquerque Monuments

   b. Major Roads

   c. City of Albuquerque

   d. Bernalillo County

You do not necessarily have to show the buffer layer. It was just a means of identifying the monuments to map. However, you have cartographers license on that choice!

2. Zoom In to the monuments layer so that you can show as much detail as possible.

3. Use the Print Composer to create a map layout.

4. Include the following map elements:

   - Title: Albuquerque Vertical Control Monuments

   - Legend

   - Your Name

   - Sources of Data

   - Scale Bar: Use the **Add Scale Bar** button 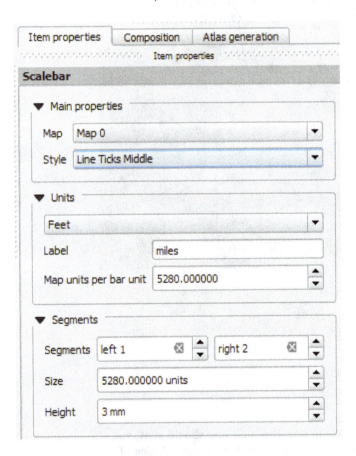. QGIS uses map units for scale bars. Here our map units are feet. Therefore, to make a scalebar read in miles you need to enter a Map units per bar unit value of 5280 (the number of feet in a mile) (Figure below).

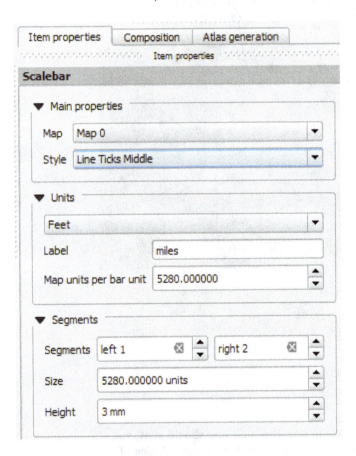

On the next page is an example of a completed map.

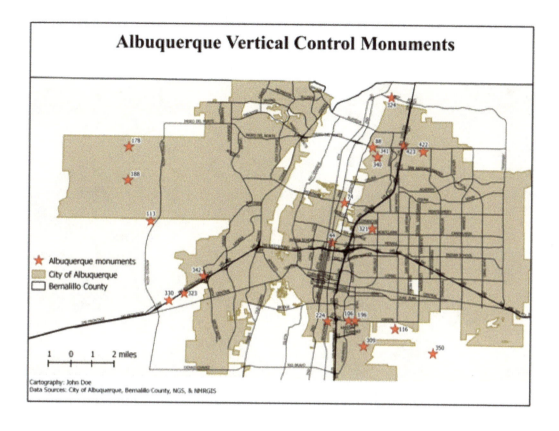

5.14   Conclusion

In this exercise, you used several basic spatial analysis techniques to prepare data for analysis and conduct the analysis. You reprojected data, queried and extracted data, conducted a dissolve operation and used buffer and clip to identify the final set of monuments. While none of these individual operations are necessarily complex, the sequence in which they were combined allowed you to answer spatial questions quickly and easily.

5.15   Discussion Questions

1. Export the final map for your instructor to grade.

2. Think of another use of a clip operation with the exercise data.

3. Could you use the dissolve tool to create a municipal boundary data set whereby all the unincorporated areas were merged together? If so describe how you would set up the tool.

5.16   Challenge Assignment (optional)

The surveyors' work was streamlined and efficient due to your GIS analysis. They now have extra time to visit The Village of Tijeras while they are in town. Generate the same analysis and accompanying map for monuments meeting the same criteria for Tijeras. You can use all the same data so you will not have to download anything else. For this map try to incorporate some of the Live Layer Effects. These can be found on the Layer Properties | Style tab under Layer rendering. Effects include: inner and outer glows and drop shadows. Visit Nyall Dawson's blog entry for more details: http://nyalldawson.net/2015/04/introducing-qgis-live-layer-effects/

Conclusion

Congratulations, you have completed the first part of GeoAcademy labs! Now that you have a good start on a well-rounded skill set, I encourage you to continue learning how QGIS, GRASS GIS, and other FOSS4G tools can be used to analyze and visualize spatial data. QGIS in particular, is undergoing rapid development with new features being introduced regularly. Below are some resources for staying abreast of the latest developments, and continuing your geospatial education.

Get the full *Discover QGIS* book from `http://locate.press` and work through all the lessons.

Learn more skills via the QGIS Training Manual: `https://www.qgis.org/en/site/forusers/trainingmaterial/index.html`

Refer to the QGIS User Manual when technical questions arise: `https://www.qgis.org/en/docs/index.html`

Subscribe to a QGIS Mailing List: `https://qgis.org/en/site/getinvolved/mailinglists.html#qgis-mailinglists`

Read about, "How to ask a QGIS question" before posing your first question to a mailing list (listserv): `https://www.qgis.org/en/site/getinvolved/faq/index.html#how-to-ask-a-qgis-question`

Read about how others have used QGIS in QGIS Case Studies: `https://www.qgis.org/en/site/about/case_studies/index.html`

Explore maps others have made using QGIS: `https://www.qgis.org/en/site/about/screenshots.html`

Read blog entries about new features and how-tos: `http://plugins.qgis.org/planet/`

Explore other QGIS Applications: `https://www.qgis.org/en/site/about/features.html`

For GRASS GIS you can visit the website to find documentation and additional tutorials, mailing lists, and other resources: `https://grass.osgeo.org/`

Visit the Open Source GeoSpatial Foundation (OSGeo) website, to stay abreast of other FOSS4G project news and conference announcements: `http://www.osgeo.org/`

Index

Books from Locate Press

QGIS Map Design

USE QGIS TO TAKE YOUR CARTOGRAPHIC PRODUCTS TO THE HIGHEST LEVEL.

With step-by-step instructions for creating the most modern print map designs seen in any instructional materials to-date, this book covers everything from basic styling and labeling to advanced techniques like illuminated contours and dynamic masking.

See how QGIS is rapidly surpassing the cartographic capabilities of any other geoware available today with its data-driven overrides, flexible expression functions, multitudinous color tools, blend modes, and atlasing capabilities. A prior familiarity with basic QGIS capabilities is assumed. All example data and project files are included.

Written by two of the leading experts in the realm of open source mapping, Anita and Gretchen are experienced authors who pour their wealth of knowledge into the book. Get ready to bump up your mapping experience!

The PyQGIS Programmer's Guide

EXTENDING QGIS JUST GOT EASIER!

This book is your fast track to getting started with PyQGIS. After a brief introduction to Python, you'll learn how to understand the QGIS Application Programmer Interface (API), write scripts, and build a plugin. The book is designed to allow you to work through the examples as you go along. At the end of each chapter you'll find a set of exercises you can do to enhance your learning experience.

The PyQGIS Programmer's Guide is compatible with the version 2.0 API released with QGIS 2.x. All code samples and data are freely available from the book's website. Get started learning PyQGIS today!

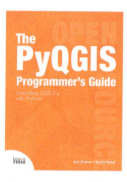

Geospatial Power Tools

EVERYONE LOVES POWER TOOLS!

The GDAL and OGR utilities are the power tools of the GIS world, and best of all, they're free.

The utilities include tools for examining, converting, transforming, building and analysing data. This book is a collection of the GDAL and OGR documentation, but also includes substantial new content designed to help guide you in using the utilities to solve your current data problems.

Inside you'll find a quick reference for looking up the right syntax and example usage quickly. The book is divided into three parts: *Workflows and examples*, *GDAL raster utilities*, and *OGR vector utilities*.

Once you get a taste of the power the GDAL/OGR suite provides, you'll wonder how you ever got along without them. This book will get you on the fast track to becoming more efficient in your GIS data processing efforts.

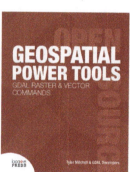

Be sure to visit http://locatepress.com for information on new and upcoming titles.

For a 50% discount on the full *Discover QGIS* PDF, see locatepress.com/dqw_pdf.   651508003a2

www.ingramcontent.com/pod-product-compliance
Lightning Source LLC
Chambersburg PA
CBHW060452060326
40689CB00020B/4501